Eighteen

all or nothing

Eighteen

all or nothing

Jennifer C Phelan

edited by
Kathryn R Bennett

First published in 2022
ISBN 9780648887607 (paperback)

Cover design by Miranda Douglas & Graham Davidson
Cover photograph 'Jennifer on Sopot Beach' © Daniel Caron
Inside cover illustration 'Jennifer's half shell' by Dayna Perez
'Polish memorabilia' photograph © Judith M Bennett
'Jen's diaries' photograph © Judith M Bennett
'Couple on beach' sketch by Nicole Perez
Internal design and typesetting by Morgan Arnett

This book is written by, and dedicated to the memory of,
Jennifer Claire Bates (née Phelan)

FOREWORD

Eighteen: All or Nothing is the diary that my daughter Jennifer kept for the twelve months that she spent as a Rotary Youth Exchange student in Warsaw, Poland. Her handwritten documents have been transcribed as written, together with copies of emails she sent to friends and relatives back home. Some names have been changed to protect identity, and bracketed clarifications have been added where needed.

The diary records Jennifer's inner journey, as well as her many travel adventures throughout Europe, during the year she turned eighteen. As you will discover, Jennifer wrote with a view to future publication. That task, however, faded from priority once she returned home and started her architecture studies at the University of Newcastle, NSW.

Prior to a trip to Warsaw in 2019 I read Jennifer's documents to prepare myself to visit some of the places that had been important to her. What I discovered was a new insight into how my daughter grew as a young woman, and how she lived, learned, loved and travelled during her year away.

My trip was, in part, a pilgrimage. In December 2016 Jennifer's life was tragically taken in a road accident. I cannot deny that preparing her diaries has formed part of my journey of grief, a privileged task that has helped ease the devastation of her loss. It has also allowed me to fulfil Jennifer's original intention of publishing her words.

Kathryn R Bennett
March 2022

ACKNOWLEDGEMENTS

Preparing Jennifer's handwritten documents to create this book has not happened without significant support and guidance.

Many of the characters in the book (all real people) have generously consented to the inclusion of Jennifer's perceptions about them, some with names changed, and others remaining identifiable.

Editing guidance has been most gratefully received to help to determine how much to cull the original documents. Typesetting and graphic design skills have shaped the final product, and Jennifer's handwriting and drawings have been digitally cleaned and prepared for insertion. Jennifer's Polish friend helped to check the Polish words throughout the diaries, and her final speech, available only in Polish, was officially translated.

The support of family and friends has enabled me to travel this journey. Daily I count my blessings for your love and encouragement. It has been a privilege to receive all your valuable assistance to bring to fruition the work that Jennifer always intended.

I have listed your names in alphabetical order as your gifts to both Jennifer and me are incomparable.

Agnieszka Maciejczak, Carole Sparkes, Daniel Caron,
Dayna Perez, Diane Heathcote, Ed Wright, Graham Davidson,
James Boggs, Jillian Kaleb, Jo Bevan, Jordi Bates, Judith Bennett,
Karen Crofts, Karin Sutton, Kenneth Phelan, Margaret Connolly,
Megan Buxton, Michelle Kelly, Miranda Douglas, Monte Dwyer,
Morgan Arnett, Nicole Perez, Olav Nemling, Philippa Ison,
Philippa Swan, Ryszard Posyniak, Scott Bevan, Simon Rosen,
Sue Whiting, Susan Francis, Suzanne Gilchrist.

Of course there is one person who does stand above everyone else
in my gratitude, my darling daughter Jennifer. As my best friend
in life, Jennifer has remained a source of support and wisdom
throughout the process of preparing her work for publication,
providing reassurance that this book is delivered with her seal of
approval. This is for you, Jen, my Favourite Female.

WHO'S WHO OF THE DIARY

(not an exclusive list)

Agata	Host mother in Żoliborz
Agnieszka	Best friend and classmate at Lelewel School
Alina	Previous Rotary exchange student to Australia
Alojzy	Host brother in Żoliborz, on Rotary exchange in Australia
Antoni	Daniel's host brother in Podkowa Leśna
Beata	Host mother in Austria, Nowak family
Brooke	Rotary exchange student from America
Carly	Rotary exchange student from America, hosted by the Nowaks in Austria
Chloe	Rotary exchange student from America
Cindy	Rotary exchange student from America
Danuta	Classmate at Lelewel School, editor of the school newspaper
Daniel	Rotary exchange student from Brazil, Jennifer's boyfriend
Ema	Daniel's host mother in Podkowa Leśna
Elena	Host sister in Austria, Nowak family
Fiona	Previous Australian Rotary exchange student to Warsaw
Gizela	Mariusz's girlfriend
Grandad	Paternal grandfather in England
Grandma	Maternal grandmother in England
Grandpa	Maternal grandfather in England
Jake	Rotary exchange student from America, travel partner to Western Europe
Janina	Host mother in Podkowa Leśna
Janiusz	Agata's friend in Żoliborz, Judyta's husband
Jaroslaw	Daniel's host father in Podkowa Leśna
Jerzy	Classmate at Lelewel School
Josef	Host father in Podkowa Leśna, Warsaw Rotarian

Judith	Maternal aunt in Australia
Judyta	Agata's friend in Żoliborz, Janiusz's wife
Julia	Host sister in Podkowa Leśna, daughter of Janina and Josef
Jackub	12-year-old host brother in Austria, Nowak family
Kasandra	Classmate at Lelewel School
Kylie	Rotary exchange student from Australia in Budapest, travel partner in Italy
Madlen	Classmate at Lelewel School
Maksym	Warsaw Rotarian
Mandek	Son of Agata's friends Judyta and Janiusz
Marcel	Classmate at Lelewel School, DJ for the school radio
Martyna	Classmate at Lelewel School
Maruisz	Employer at children's summer camp and English teaching classes
Marysia	Antoni's sister, Rotary exchange student to Australia
Miranda	Host sister in Żoliborz, studying in Helsinki
Nana	Paternal grandmother in England
Nowak	Host family in Austria
Olek	Host father in Austria, Nowak family. Warsaw Rotarian
Oskar	16-year-old host brother in Austria, Nowak family
Paweł	Classmate at Lelewel School
Philippa	Australian school friend
Pip	Friend in England
Pieter	Alojzy's best friend in Żoliborz
Ron	Australian District Rotarian
Simon	Boyfriend of Pip in England
Terry	Rotary exchange student from America
Tymon/Tym	Former Rotary exchange student to Australia
Walenty	Host father in Żoliborz
Wicek	Warsaw Rotarian

All or Nothing became a motto
of my one-year visit to Poland.

And thanks to that motto I have
accomplished my objectives.

Jennifer C Phelan
1999

Żoliborz

[Warsaw]

6.55 am Monday 19 January 1998

Wow. Am I really here?

Morning is beginning to dawn on leafless Warsaw as I reflect on the incredible 48 hours that have just passed. Exactly 48 hours ago I was standing with Mum and Dad in the baggage check-in line at Sydney airport, dressed in my Rotary uniform, calm but nervous. Group photos were taken, then it was time to wade through the sea of sobbers and enter the customs area. A last hug, a brave wave and we parted. We boarded the largest work of modern art in the world – the QANTAS jet covered in Aboriginal designs.

As I walked through the doors into the arrivals lounge in Warsaw, a pair of arms enfolded me – it was my first host mother. Next to her was my host father. From the other side, my Rotary counsellor stepped forward, spoke to me in English and gave me a T-shirt. I was then introduced to Karina and Anita, exchange students from Brazil, and two American boys. Pieter, Alojzy's best friend, was there also.

'Do you feel overwhelmed?' asked one of the American boys. 'Yes,' I answered – that summed it up very well.

I got a tour of Warsaw on the way home. Pieter pointed things out to me and spoke to me in English. I spotted the house from the street as I had seen it before in Alojzy's photos. I am staying in Alojzy's room. I just had time to unpack all my things and get changed before tea was ready. As I was doing so, I found little messages in various things that Mummy had put there.

After tea we had a photo fest. I showed my host parents the photos of Alojzy, and my two photo albums. They showed me pictures of Alojzy in France, Alojzy in Turkey, Alojzy in Greece and Alojzy in Cobar, Australia. It was clear to see that they were missing him.

I then went with my host mum, Agata, to take Pieter home and got the tour of the city by night. The Vistula, the large solid-looking buildings, the neon signs, the fairy lights, the monuments, the people, the cars, the wedding cake building [the Palace of Culture]. Mind-blowing. We went past the Opera House, and Agata told me she has tickets for Saturday.

When we returned, I took a shower, phoned Mum and Dad and went to bed very happy. Here beginneth the adventure.

19-1-98

A purple postman, moustaches, flocks of blackbirds, shop assistants on roller skates, orange capsicum and live fish in the supermarket. Just some of the things I have seen on my first day in Warsaw.

22-1-98

My first day at school was GREAT. I am at Lelewel School in class 3A, which consists of 5 boys and about 20 girls. They are all so very friendly and excited to have an Australian in their class for a year. They all spoke to me in English, so I didn't get to practice my Polish; but never mind.

Each class has a cloakroom in the basement. The first and second lessons were in Polish. The class is studying a 500-page crime novel which they had two weeks to read. The Polish teacher is not well-liked by 3A. They think she is very boring and they miss their former teacher who is now the *Dyrektor*.

Next was gym. I had to watch since I didn't take a change of clothes. I got talking to Danuta, who doesn't participate in gym because of her knees. She's nice. Between lessons everyone flocks to the common area near the front of the school and the school radio blares from the speakers. One of the boys in 3A is a DJ for the radio. Danuta is involved in the school magazine and asked me to write an article for it. I gladly agreed. Another good friend I made today is Agnieszka. She is very smart, very helpful and eager to learn about Australia. She said we might go to the movies together one day.

After gym we had *matamatyka*. I could understand this subject much easier. After this, half the class went to do a maths test which they had to repeat because they didn't pass last time. Meanwhile I went with the others to religion. The priest leads this class. He generously gave me some picture cards and magazines to look at while the others did a test. During this, he played his guitar and sang along. The test finished at about 12.50 pm, and it was time to go home.

The students don't like the school buildings with their peeling paint and dullness, but I believe this is not as important as the people who create the community feeling, and it is certainly a very friendly atmosphere. I hope their friendliness continues after I cease to be a novelty.

Yesterday I took my first trip on a Warsaw tram. I explored a bit more of Warsaw centre, including the wedding cake building and the markets in front of it, then managed to get home by myself. I find this rather ironic – that I get lost getting around Sydney in my country, yet have no problem getting around the capital city of a foreign country. A stranger even asked me the time (without the aid of mime), and I understood her.

23-1-98

Well, I christened my leather jacket last night. I wore it to a concert of the Warsaw Philharmonic orchestra. Sounds impressive, hey?

Everyone is saying how well I speak Polish. I met Tymon, the former exchange student to Australia, for the first time yesterday, and he was astonished at my progress given the short amount of time that I have been here. He said that I am the first Australian exchange student to Poland who is making an effort to learn the language. Even my school friends are impressed that I want to learn Polish. Agnieszka from school told me that her dad thought I was a Polish girl when I rang her house the other night.

I am determined to change the Australian stereotype of slack-arsed whingers and prove that we are not all like that.

1-2-98

Whoops, I've let my writing lapse. I've just been so busy. The many jaunts of this past week have been WOW.

I'll begin with last Saturday, the night when I had three invitations to three different events. I managed to squeeze two of those in – Terry's party [an exchange student from America] and Lelewel's *studniowka* [a ball for final grade high school students] – but couldn't get to the opera with Mama. She said that was OK because Walenty, my host father, would go instead and we could go another time.

So I had to be in Felinica at 4 pm, and we were taking the Brazilian girls with us. We had a problem though – the phone wasn't working so I couldn't contact Karina to tell her we were going to be late. As we were approaching Terry's street, we passed the two Brazilian girls sitting at a bus stop. We backed up, and they told us they were waiting for Terry's host mum who was supposed to meet them at 4 pm and it was now 4.15 pm. They jumped in the back seat, and we continued. At the next bus stop, there was Terry's host mum waiting in the car. It was quite hilarious. I don't know what would have happened if we hadn't come along.

It was the first time I'd met the other exchange students in a casual setting. We chatted, ate, and listened to music. I particularly talked with Jake (the nineteen-year-old from Oregon), and he told me about his upcoming trip of Western Europe with a friend who was flying out from the States. He realised that I was interested so said that he would check with his friend and see if I could come along.

At about 7 pm we all left to catch a bus into the city, and I caught another bus to Żoliborz to attend the party at school. I got there in perfect timing, 8.50 pm. I found Agnieszka and her sister and soon we were watching the 4th Class do the traditional *Polonaise* dance they had been practising for so many weeks. The decorations looked fabulous. The whole place was re-created into a scene from the Old Town, sheets of painted paper covered the walls from floor to ceiling, and blue and white balloons hung in bunches from walls, ceilings and pillars. Even the supper rooms were fully decorated – this time with dragons.

Supper was served after the *Polonaise*. This was the time that most of the parents left and let the students enjoy themselves. The band cranked up, and the dancing began. Agnieszka introduced me to some former students of Lelewel – three guys who are now at university and one of which was Danuta's boyfriend. Unfortunately, Danuta couldn't be there because she was studying. While we were dancing the *Dyrektor* came over and introduced me to Liam from Australia. He's from Melbourne and here in Poland for a holiday where he's staying with family because he's half Polish. It was great to hear an Australian accent. We chatted for a while and then went back to dancing. Unfortunately Agnieszka had to leave at midnight. I stayed and continued dancing with the new people I'd met and later I found Liam again. He asked me to dance one of the slow dances and at 5 am he walked me home (very romantic). He invited me to go with him to visit cousins of his that day. I accepted the invitation, and he said he would call at 9.30 am.

He kept his promise. We caught the bus to a village on the outskirts of Warsaw. Chrystian, his cousin, met us and we walked to a little pub on the edge of a forest. There were seven of us in all – Chrystian and partner (married three weeks ago), Chrystian's friend and partner, Chrystian's sister and Liam and me. We had traditional Polish hot beer and then went walking in the forest. It was a perfect day – only a couple of degrees in temperature but a clear blue sky and a beautiful freshness about the air.

After this, we went to Chrystian' house for *obiad*, the main meal of the day. They live in quite a large house with beautiful views over the fields. Chrystian showed us a passionate interest of his – composing music on computer. Then we ate – boy did we eat, it was delicious.

It was about 4 pm at this stage – time to start thinking about leaving. Chrystian drove us home. There was no-one home at my house, so I had to go to Liam's place for an hour or so before I met Agnieszka at 5.30 pm. (What a shame!)

I went to Mass that evening with Agnieszka at a local modern church. It was packed. I found it rather difficult to keep my eyes open – after all, I had only had 2 hours sleep in the last 36 hours, and the Mass was in Polish. It was an interesting experience none-the-less. Afterwards, I went back to Agnieszka's apartment, where she showed me photos of her trips to various countries in Europe.

And that was my first weekend in Poland.

Monday was Australia Day. I hadn't had time to make a carrot cake, so instead, I quickly made some vegemite sandwiches, arranged them in the shape of Australia and stuck flags in each one then took it to school. In our homeroom lesson I told everyone of the significance of Australia Day and passed around the sandwiches.

In the evening I was supposed to be going to the T-Love concert, but it had been cancelled; a girl was murdered at the venue on Saturday, and the club was closed. This was rather shocking. I stayed home and wrote letters instead.

After school on Tuesday, I met Jake at the uni. We went to get my ID card and then to the pub. We got out the map and started talking about travel. We planned the itinerary, then went back to the uni so I could email it to Mum and Dad. We arranged to meet again the following day to check the mail. This, however, did not work out. I got home, realised school finished later the next day but couldn't phone Jake because the phone was out of order. So the next day I got to the meeting place 1½ hours late, and of course, he wasn't there. I decided to hang around until the Rotary meeting but never quite got there because I had my first experience of being lost in Warsaw. I couldn't for the life of me remember where the Rotary club venue was. I tried to phone home for directions, but of course, the phone wasn't working. I gave up and decided to catch the bus home. I got on the wrong bus. I ended up west when I was meant to be north with a bus driver who couldn't speak English. Thankfully he took me to where I could catch a bus home. Finally, I got home.

After school on Thursday, Liam came for lunch. We looked at photos, and he read my article for the school magazine. I went with him to the bus stop at 4 pm, and I will probably never see him again. At 5 pm I met Agnieszka and another friend of hers, and we went ice skating at the local outdoor rink. It was quite fun. For Agnieszka, she was reliving a part of her childhood.

After school on Friday, I went shopping in Centrum with a different group of girls from my class. I'm starting to work out where everyone stands in the class, and I think these girls are the rich and popular ones with boyfriends, and they smoke. It was nice of them to invite me, and even though I didn't buy anything, it was a nice outing.

I've been talking a lot about what I have been doing after school every day, but school itself has been great also. Marcel, the school DJ, is eager for me to listen to Polish rock music and has lent me tapes of his favourite band Voo Voo. I did a talk on Aborigines the other day. I've been helping the class with their English, and they have been helping me with Polish.

Saturday morning I met Jake at the Rotunda at 8.15 am. We were off to Katowice for the Genesis concert. Abby [an American exchange student] had dropped out, so it was only the two of us. The train trip was 2½ hours through serene white countryside. We got to Katowice at about noon with no idea of what the city had to offer. In short, there is not much to do in Katowice, but it was a bit of an adventure. We found a pub to spend the remaining hour and discussed travel again. Jake told me on the phone on Friday that his friend would rather not have anyone along on the trip. So I am now considering meeting Jake after Oliver has left, and doing Ireland, Spain, Southern France and Venice in three weeks.

We left the pub at 4.50 pm for the concert venue, where we stood with everyone else in the queue for an hour in the cold. The doors opened at 6, and we got our position on the floor and stood for another 2 hours. The band finally appeared at 8 pm. The concert was great – the first tour of Genesis with their new lead singer. I recognised about 5 or 6 songs. The drum kit was fabulous – I want one.

We had 5 hours to kill before our train. We both just wanted to find somewhere to sit that was warm. We finally found a pub. We had a few beers and ate the sandwiches I had brought. Unfortunately, they kicked us out at 2 am – we still had two hours to go. We went to the train station and sat in the café by the heater – the favourite place of all the yobbos in town it seemed. It was difficult to stay awake.

On my way back from the toilet I was chased by the toilet lady. I couldn't understand what she was saying to me, but Jake told me that she wanted 80 groszy for using the toilet. I couldn't believe that she'd come after me for an amount that was about 26 cents, Australian.

I managed about an hour's sleep on the train, and we pulled into Warsaw as a new day was dawning. At 8 am I was ringing the doorbell. It was quite a fun adventure, I thought.

I forgot to mention that Warsaw is now white. It snowed for the first time – I think it was Tuesday. I walked to school saying (ironically), 'Zipadee do da zipadee ay, my oh my what a wonderful day.'

My life is a whirlwind. I feel like I'm grasping to keep up with my own life. For example, the afternoons for the coming week are already booked. Jake says it's great that I'm out and about so soon and I agree. Jake has been so good to me. He has made it his business to make sure I have everything I need and is someone I can talk to about feelings and ideas. Anyway, if Saturday was anything to go by I think he will be a great travelling companion.

Contrary to popular belief, I love my school and the friends I have in 3A. These friends are dearer to me than my exchange friends (other than Jake).

3-2-98

Yesterday's jaunt took me to Radio 3 – a national government radio station situated on the other side of Warsaw. Agnieszka, Magdalena, Marcel, two others and I were taken there by the journalist who has us for two lessons every second Monday. The other five participated in a chat show about school education in Poland. Meanwhile I watched through the window from the control room, and partway through was taken for a tour of the station by this journalist who also speaks English. It was fantastic. Also present for the show were the Minister and Vice-Minister for Education. Agnieszka and the others disagreed with his views and Magdalena even said some things against teachers in Poland. So today many of the teachers had words with her.

Today we had an excursion to a renaissance art exhibition in the Winter Palace in the Old Town. After this, some of us went to see a modern exhibition of photography by Annie Leibovitz in the Summer Palace. Both were great. It was quite a cultural day today. I commented to Danuta on the way to the Palace that the bus trip was a cultural experience for me because it was packed like a tin of sardines. Then, on the path to the Palace, we were running and sliding on the snow. Danuta turned around and said, 'Another cultural experience for you.' And we also had a snowball fight this afternoon on our way to the Summer Palace. It was great fun.

7-2-98

The journey of introspection and defining self has begun. I suppose I've always known I am a person of variety – variety in music, food, interests, etc. but it's only now that I'm beginning to accept that this is a good thing, rather than feeling like I lack the power of distinction. I've realised that it means I can have friends from a vast array of interest backgrounds.

Well, what have I been doing since I last wrote? Thursday I took the day off school because two lessons had been cancelled leaving only Polish and W.F [Physical Education]. I decided to make a pavlova as Agnieszka was coming for *obiad*. The pavlova didn't work, so we had fruit salad instead. After this, she took me shopping in central Warsaw – Nowy Świat. I bought a beret, a pair of jeans, a shirt, some writing paper, a Valentine's card and some postcards. It was great. Agnieszka generously gave up her afternoon to be my guide and interpreter – she is sooo nice. I met Terry and Jake at the Rotunda at 6 pm, and we went to see *Sweet Hereafter* at one of the many cinemas in Warsaw. Brilliant film, one that makes you think, and the great thing was talking about it and analysing it afterwards with Terry and Jake. It's a great feeling to throw around ideas, viewpoints and what you got out of it with two intelligent people. We went to Piast for an hour or so where a Polish guy was playing and singing Beatles' songs.

Friday was the last day of school before two weeks of winter holiday. No-one was in the mood for schoolwork. I wrote a letter, and when I got home, I wrote a few more. Katryna gave me a bunch of photocopied pages on Polish grammar and Mina a book on Polish grammar. They're such helpful people. Everyone played truant on the last lesson.

I hoped Jake might call that night because we had talked about me going to his place on Saturday. He didn't. I didn't want to phone him because it would seem like I was inviting myself. It was a really stupid thing to do when I look back on it now, and I don't know what I'm going to say to Jake when I speak to him next.

At 5.30 pm on Saturday, Pieter came to pick me up. We went to his place, and he got ready for the *studniowka*, then he and his mother and I got a taxi to his school. The decorations were fabulous – designed by Pieter. The theme was a medieval dungeon. Brown paper covered the walls, and army netting hung from the roof. The lights were covered in coloured crepe paper to give it an eerie atmosphere. The gym, where the dancing took place, had its walls covered in silver paper and blue and white balloons from the netting. So, compared with the Lelewel *studniowka*, the decorations were about of the same standard.

Unlike at Lelewel, where everyone in the Fourth Year did the Polonaise at the same time, each of the three classes performed the Polonaise separately. The first floor corridors were decked with long tables full of all kinds of food – meat, bread, salads, cakes, sweets, fruit, etc. The food was better than at Lelewel. Pieter's *studniowka* did not have a band, so from that aspect, Lelewel was better as it had both a band and DJ who alternated. Like Lelewel, there was also a series of skits performed halfway through the evening. For me, last night's performances were better than at Lelewel because it was more visual. And then there was the dancing. And they did a very good job. I think the standard here was better than Lelewel.

I danced with Pieter and about three of his friends. It was so much fun. Polish guys are so much better at dancing than Australian guys. (Not that I've ever really experienced dancing with Australian guys – the problem with Australian guys is that they're just too lazy. Or maybe it's the age thing. I like nineteen-year-old guys.) Anyway, *było fajnie* [it was cool]. I got home at 6.30 am.

I've noticed that I've learnt very quickly the Polish words for things like 'good', 'beautiful', 'great' and things of the future, e.g. 'tomorrow', but I don't know words that describe anything bad or in the past. This just goes to show that everything so far has been fantastic and that I'm usually forward-thinking.

11-2-98

Last night Mummy rang with my PIN for phone calls. I called her back to test it then I called Grandma and Grandpa to tell them of my travel plans. They are very excited that I will be visiting them very shortly, but I could sense the shock and surprise in their voices when I told them I'd be travelling Europe with Jake. I can see it from their point of view, which is possibly Mum and Dad's view also; their only daughter/granddaughter is about to embark on a pretty big trip around Europe with a nineteen-year-old American boy who she only met 3½ weeks ago.

The way I look at it though is that it is an unmissable opportunity – not only to travel to some of the places I want to go to but to travel with someone who has similar priorities and zest for life. I see it as an opportunity to develop a friendship (I mean friendship, not relationship) through travel rather than developing a friendship to ascertain whether you want to travel with that person. Maybe this is a dangerous way of doing things, but we did spend 23 hours in each other's company when we went to Katowice (only apart for trips to the toilet), and I said back then that if this trip was anything to go by I think he will be a great travelling companion. I am confident about it. After all, my motto is:

'Do it, be it, live it.'

Kraków

15-2-98

Things were beginning to cease being wow... and then we came to Kraków. Although the weather has been pretty miserable, what I've seen of this beautiful old city shows why it has the reputation it does. This evening, like last evening, we are spending at Agata's sister's place, and again I've eaten too much.

Have I been here four weeks already? It seems like only two. Time is going so fast.

16-2-98

I've decided I don't like guys paying for me when I go out. It's as if it's payment for what they want later. This is how it felt when I went out with Tymon anyhow. This experience has been on my mind for the past few days, but it's only now that I feel ready to write about it. We had planned to go ice-skating on Thursday evening, but due to the weather, we went to Centrum instead.

The more we talked, the more I realised that we just didn't gel, not even as friends. He's sexist (thinks women shouldn't play ice-hockey or be in the police force) and identifies with a sub-culture that Agnieszka has warned me about. He didn't try to make any move on me, but I know he likes me, and the problem is I don't know what to do. He kept saying he'd love to go to Australia, he wishes he was in Australia, and he can imagine himself lazing on the beach all day. I may be wrong, but this gives me the impression that he sees me as his ticket out of Poland. This is definitely something I've never experienced before. It wouldn't be so bad if I were only here for 12 weeks, but I'm here for 12 months, and he lives in the same city. He might be a good dancer, but that doesn't mean anything. I have resolved to talk to Pieter about it.

19-2-98

'Forever young, I want to be, forever young.' The words of the song that was playing on the radio. Quite appropriate. Yes, I'm still enjoying myself immensely – meeting new people, discovering new places. I think it is this 'newness' and lack of routine that keeps me alive.

Writing in this book has been neglected lately in preference to email. Yesterday I sent a whole batch of epic emails describing the trip to Kraków and various other things. Hopefully Mum and Dad will save my emails so if this is ever published the email sent on 18-2-98 should be slotted in here.

From: jennifer phelan
To: Mum and Dad
Subject: Kraków
Date: Thursday, 19 February 1998

Hi there.

We returned from Kraków earlier than I expected. There, waiting for me on
my desk when I got home, were all three of your letters plus one each from
grandparents. I was so overwhelmed with excitement I didn't know which to
open first. Thank you so much. Most Q's have been answered in subsequent
phone conversations and my last email. The [newspaper] article on Alojzy
and me is fantastic. Agata and Walenty love it too and have taken it to make
copies. The photo original will be a great gift for them. Thank you for the
letter of consent. I'll take it in tonight. Thanks too for the school newsletter –
Jillian 3rd in the state for Ancient History – wow. I'll take it to school next
week – I'm sure my class will be very interested to see it, particularly Danuta.

And thank you for the CD and postcards – great idea. I was so high with
adrenaline that I lay in bed for hours before I could get to sleep last night.

So, the trip to Kraków. Great apart from the weather. Drove down on
Friday (six hours by car but three hours by train). We stayed in Miranda's
apartment, which is situated right near the entrance to Wawel Castle. I don't
know why she would want to go and study in Helsinki when she has an
apartment like that – it's fabulous. Agata's sister, Edyta, lives in the same
block. Agata and Edyta own the three apartment blocks.

On Saturday, they had some business to do concerning the accounts of the
apartments. Meanwhile, Agata's friends Judyta and Janiusz and I visited
Wawel. I joined a tour in English for part of the church tour. We went up the
tower that houses the famous Zigismund Bell. Unfortunately, there was not

much of a view. The city was shrouded in a thick mist from which emerged the eerie sounds of the lone trumpeter heralding the hour. Outside the castle, we saw the statue of Kosciuszko and a statue of the mythical Kraków dragon. In the afternoon, Agata drove us to Wieliczka (20 minutes), home of the world's oldest salt mine. Three of the 300 kilometres of tunnel are opened to tourists. The tour begins with steps which take you down about 160 metres (a long way). We saw amazing salt sculptures, two salt lakes and an incredible chapel with biblical events carved into the salt walls and crystal salt chandeliers hanging from the ceiling. Agata tricked me into believing we would have to climb the steps to get out again, but of course, there was a lift. I felt at home. Not only is Agata generous, understanding and kind but also has a great sense of fun. She often says to me, 'Come on my Jennifer, my little daughter.' She gives me hugs too.

Saturday evening we went to a traditional old-style Polish restaurant. Great atmosphere, great food and three musicians in the corner singing songs about love (it was Valentine's Day which is a big thing in Poland). To begin, they brought out slices of bread and two rustic mugs on a rustic breadboard. In one mug was a cheese spread and the other a pork spread. Main course was *pierogi* – mini dumplings filled with either cabbage, potatoes and cheese or mince. Self-serve salads of carrot, cabbage and gherkins. I drank spring water with jam.

Sunday we got up early and went to Zakopane. Unfortunately, the amount of snow was minimal, so skiing was off. Plus the rain was steady and continual. We began our visit with Mass in the famous wooden church built by the mountain people in dedication to the Pope. We walked the main street and tried mountain sheep cheese. Took a short walk at the base of one of the ski-fields where there was some snow and a pretty mountain stream. Houses are of a very distinctive architectural style in the mountains – steep-roofed, veranda-less and made of stone and wood.

Unlike Warsaw, Kraków was not destroyed during the war, so the buildings are original. There is a fabulous atmosphere and a real sense of the old. This can be found in Warsaw too, but it is restricted to the Old Town which is then surrounded by the busy commerciality of a major European city. In Kraków, churches are almost every 100 metres, and within them, confessional boxes are about every 10 metres. There are always people inside praying, gazing or confessing. They are truly splendid works of art.

On Monday, Agata had more business, so Judyta, Janiusz and I went souvenir shopping in the famous Cloth Hall in the market square. It is lined with little stalls selling traditional Polish arts and crafts.

True to 'Murphy's Law', the weather was perfect for the day we had to return. Blue sky, sunshine and cool, crisp, clean air and we had to spend it in the car! I'm glad though that I've seen Kraków in that weather because it's certain I will go again, probably in spring and I guess it will look totally different in different weather.

From Kraków, we brought back with us Miranda's computer. I've set it up in my room, and Pieter (Alojzy's best friend) is coming over this afternoon to get it working for me (he's a computer whizz). Hopefully, I will then be able to compose emails at home, save them to disk, take the disk to the internet café and do a copy-paste job to save cost. I'll also be able to use the computer for writing my article about music because the most common question I've been asked is, 'What type of music do you like?' There doesn't seem to be anyone like me who likes a bit of everything – they all seem to identify with one style only.

My pimples are back! My forehead has suddenly broken out. This could be due to a number of reasons. The wearing of a beret almost every day. The lack of exercise – I'm keen to get out on Alojzy's bike, but every time I'm ready it rains. Or the diet – high in protein and carbohydrate and low in fresh fruit and vegetables. The typical meals for a day are fish, meat or sausage with bread for breakfast. Then there is what they call second breakfast about 11 am, which is usually an apple and a sandwich. The timing of the main meal varies depending on what we're doing but is usually about 3 pm, and we eat meat (chicken, sausage etc.) with potatoes, pasta, rice or *kasza* [buckwheat] and either salad or vegetables. Supper is whatever you want at about 7 pm. It might be fruit, bread, *pierogi*, cake etc. Polish cakes are absolutely more-ish. There is one particular one called *pączek* which is like a sweet bun filled with rose jam and glazed with a light sticky icing. I'm contemplating the logistics of bringing some to England – you've just got to try them.

In Kraków, we had supper with Edyta, and she had these little more-ish devils. I happened to express how much I liked them so the next day when I was shopping with Judyta and Janiusz, they bought me one for morning tea. Then when we got home, we discovered that Agata had bought a box full so I had to have one for lunch and supper. The diet starts today! The only food I miss is soya milk.

Today is the 18th of March, I've been here exactly a month, yet it feels like only two weeks. So much has happened but so quickly. In honour of this, I'm going to make stir fry and carrot cake for Agata and Walenty on Saturday and present them with my gifts. It looks like I'll be having only two host families and changing in June or July. Seeing as how I bought gifts for four they'll get double.

I spoke briefly to Alojzy on the phone last night (please note the spelling, you both got it wrong). The reason he hasn't contacted you lately is because he lost your number. He has it now, and I told him you'd love to hear from him. Agata's sister and friends were very keen to know what I thought of Alojzy. I said I liked him and that he is very funny and that you both like him very much. Then they joked about setting us up together at a party when he returns. They don't realise how much I understand Polish. It doesn't bother

me the constant chatter in Polish, sometimes I switch off but if I concentrate
I can understand a fair bit. Yes, there are regional dialects as I discovered
when we went to Zakopane. Agata told me that the mountain people speak
quite differently – understandable but different. It's funny how many Polish
words have been adopted from English. See if you can guess the origin of
these words:

interesujące
absolutny
oryginalny
normalny
naturalny
super (this one isn't hard)

Before we went to Kraków, I bought some brown oiled leather walking boots
from the Warsaw markets. They are sheepskin lined and cost the equivalent
of A$40. Speaking of money, my total expenditure for this month has been
about $320. This doesn't include the pocket money from Rotary which works
out at about $14 a week. How do you think I should budget for my trip?

I keep finding your little messages and packages hidden in my things –
thank you so much. The funny thing is I tend to discover them when I'm
at the height of happiness, and they give me an extra kick, and I think I'm
going to explode. I want to thank you again for putting on the farewell party
for me. It is a very happy memory I will carry with me forever.

Alojzy was right about the extent to which Polish people smoke, particularly
young people. Agata goes down to the basement when she needs a
cigarette but unfortunately the laundry and the smoking room are one and
the same thing so even though she doesn't smoke in my presence, my
clothes always smell of smoke anyway.

Public toilets in Poland rarely have toilet paper in the cubicles. You have to collect it from a person at the door when you enter, and often you have to pay for it. This is something I've had to get used to. Who'd want to be a toilet paper monitor though?

This has been an epic and will cost me about A$7. Pass on the good news, and please write. Good luck with the preparations. Will Kelly be housesitting? If you can't get me a Eurail pass, I can probably get one when I get to England.

Lots of love,

Jennifer xxx

Żoliborz

19-2-98

Events of today have opened my mind concerning the issue I wrote about last time. I saw the movie *Chasing Amy* with Agnieszka, which looks at the problems faced by minority groups from the inside. It mainly focuses on homosexuals but also looks at Negroes. It was a very interesting, clever and thought-provoking film – I feel as if I still need time to think it over again. This, coupled with the conversation I had this evening about sub-cultures, made me realise that I was being prejudiced against Tymon because he identified with the subculture called *'dres'* [similar to 'bogan' or 'chav'] of which I have had no first-hand experience, only a second-hand warning. I know the other thing that bothered me about him was that he's sexist – is it prejudice to judge someone based on their prejudice?

I did discuss this issue, rather awkwardly, with Pieter as I said I would, last evening when he came to set up the computer. He told me not to worry – Tym will probably forget to call, and his manner suggested I was making a big deal of nothing. Maybe I am. And if he does call, I can easily accept or reject any invitation depending on what's on offer.

From: jennifer phelan
To: Mum and Dad
Subject: Re: M&D News
Date: Saturday, 21 February 1998

Dear Mummy and Daddy,

I sit typing this in the comfort of my bedroom thanks to Pieter who set up
the system like a professional setterupperer! He's heading for a career in
computers. It is quite funny navigating my way around the Polish version of
Windows 95 – everything is in the same place just written in Polish – so it
is a good way of learning the Polish words for things like file and help etc.
Interestingly I can type in English, and it still corrects the spelling – Microsoft
Word must be multi-language compatible. Pieter told me that the Polish
spell checker's alternative for my name is Renifer which means reindeer. So
guess what my new nickname is?

In one of your letters, you asked me to tell you about my morning routine.
Well, I have my shower at night because I wash my hair every second night
and dry it with the hairdryer. When I get up, I put my many layers of clothes
on, eat breakfast alone, pack my second breakfast, wash my face, brush my
teeth and go to school. Agata and Walenty are late to bed and late to rise
people so often I don't even see them in the mornings. Even though the
mornings are cold and my bed is warm, I haven't yet felt the desire to stay in
bed – I'm usually eager to embrace whatever adventures the day has in store
for me. Neither have I felt really cold. I find the Poles complaining of the cold
because they are not wearing enough clothes. I wear a singlet, a spencer, a
skivvy, a shirt, a jumper (or two) and then when I go outside I put on scarf,
beret, gloves and Alojzy's beautiful down jacket. The leggings are great –
please tell Auntie Doris and Mary that my legs are very happy in them. The
camera is fantastic too – it goes everywhere with me in my Fiorelli handbag.
I'm so glad we went for compactness because by having it with me always,

I get the spontaneous shots I might not have otherwise captured if I had
a large camera to lug around. The reason that the first two films weren't
brilliant quality is perhaps because I was using the 400ASA films we bought
for me to practice with before I left Australia. I now have a 200ASA film in.
They are on the whole good pictures though, with great memories attached.

Could you please send me some more of the small packets of eucalyptus
lollies? I found them great to share at school. In one of the geography
lessons, I was asked to point on the map to where the forests are in
Australia and say what type of forest it is. It is very funny trying to teach a
Polish person how to say yoo-cal-yp-tus! A difficult sound for Polish people
to pronounce in English is 'th.' Can you think of any tongue twisters based
on 'th'? Some of my friends have been trying to teach me Polish tongue
twisters. The sound that I have trouble with is 'trz', but I can cope with the
'cz', 'sz', etc.

Are you ready for the tale of my next amusing mishap with words? This
morning Walenty, Agata and I went to register me as an extra occupant
of the house. On our return, I wanted to ask if I could buy some wrapping
paper. In Polish, the words for paper and cigarettes are very similar.

Need I say more?

There are throwbacks from the Communist era that I'm discovering. It is
very easy to get lost on a site of many apartment blocks as they all look
the same – tall, grey and solid. Many of the people who I've talked to who
live in apartments don't like it and dream of having their own house in the
suburbs. Something else is the ritual of collecting water from the communal
well. I went with Agata the other day and was fascinated. We take the crate
of empty plastic bottles to this small hut situated near the shopping centre.
Inside there are taps lining two walls and people filling their bottles in a
manner that shows they have been doing it for years.

Thanks heaps for your very entertaining email – I will save to disk, take it home and read it over and over. The next time I will be here will be Tuesday afternoon (Wed morning for you).

Love you and leave you

Renifer!

23-2-98

I've had so many thoughts but not enough time to record them. This is turning into a thoughts diary, and my emails are the events diaries. I want to discuss maturity. I have now heard many stories about Nick, the sixteen-year-old American exchange student, who should still be here but he couldn't cope and went home after, I think, three months. He was staying with Agata and Walenty. Funnily enough, when I picture his name, for some reason, I see it without the 'k' which transforms it into the Polish word for 'nothing'. Perhaps significant. Anyway, most of the people I am meeting through Agata met Nick, so naturally, I am compared with him. Everyone says how much more mature I am compared with him. They are surprised and impressed that I don't feel homesick, afraid or alone.

This evening I had an interesting conversation with Miranda and her friends about maturity from a different angle. Yet in my head, the train of thought led to this comparison between Nick and I. It began with a comment from one of Miranda's friends, that compared with Polish girls of my age, Australian girls are much more mature. I said that he can't generalise about Australian girls based solely on me and that in any case, I believe that maturity is an individual thing – nothing to do with nationality. So, Nick's immaturity is a result of self not because he is American. Jake, although he is three years older, proves this point. For example, this evening on the phone I asked him how his holiday in Italy was. Rather than talk for ages about it like someone I used to know would have done, he said it was great and immediately asked me how I enjoyed Kraków.

Polish people don't make idle promises. If they invite you somewhere, they will call to confirm the time and place, or even pick you up. I'm still finding it hard to believe how willing my new friends are to take me places. It's truly incredible – it's as if this entire network of friends were just waiting here for me to uncover. I'm very glad that I have approached my year with the attitude of optimism and open-mindedness even though some of the things I wrote in January tended towards the self-righteous. It has, and is, truly paying off. This extends to drinking the occasional beer because it is very much part of the culture here and, as I explained to Agata this evening, I promised myself to participate in every facet of Polish culture as long as it wasn't hurting anyone. For instance, picture this, sitting in the pub, everyone with a beer in front of them except me. It's called sticking out like a sore thumb!

Here I am at the end of my diary [Journeys and Jaunts], and I've only been here for five weeks. It's very surprising how I've felt this urgent need to write down these feelings, thoughts and ideas, not only to preserve them for the future but also to empty my head of them before a collision between a feeling and a thought begins WW3 in my mind. Agata must think I'm sending Morse code to someone across the street considering the number of times I've turned my lamp on and off tonight.

3-3-98

wszystko albo nic

I haven't decided yet whether this is going to be my motto for March or my motto in Polish to balance my motto in English, which is 'Do it, Be it, Live it'.

This all came about as a result of my trip to TPS television studios to watch the recording of the Polish game show with this title – *All or Nothing*. I went last night with Pieter who got us in due to his connections. For Pieter it wasn't as engaging as perhaps a comedy show or a music show, but for me, because it was based on actions, it was very entertaining. I enjoyed watching all the people in the studio going about their tasks, and the engineers in the mixing room. I brought home with me a souvenir flag with the show's name on it which symbolises for me a turning point in a dull patch I was going through – hence the lapse in writing. Last time I wrote was after getting back from the pub where I had been with Miranda and her friends – that was Monday night.

On Tuesday, Jake came to my house, and we spent 5 hours organising the itinerary for our trip. Then Grandma rang and said she'd prefer it if we deferred our stay in Leeds until Mum and Dad had settled in and were over their jet lag, and that she was not too keen on Jake staying there. However, when I was in the shower I had a brainwave – we should go to Ireland before Leeds rather than the other way around as previously planned. I put this to Jake at the Rotary meeting on Wednesday night, and he agreed as long as we had accommodation and transport. I said I would work on it. Grandma rang again as promised. I put my proposition to her and got agreement. I immediately rang Pip [a family friend in Bristol] who, without hesitation, said she would take two days off work to drive us around, and would investigate transit buses from Heathrow to Bristol for us. I was so overjoyed I pranced around the house. I delivered the good news to Jake in a phone call the following day. However, my elation was not to last long.

For the third consecutive night, Grandma phoned. 'Don't you think you are trying to do too much? You are only seventeen; don't you think you should be spending more time with your Grandparents because frankly, we don't know how many more opportunities we'll have. I'm not trying to put a damper on your plans, but...' Such was the gist of her monologue. It was after this phone call that I cried for the first time since arriving in Poland. A cocktail of tiredness and PMS, which was made volatile by the selfish tone of Grandma's voice over the telephone. I was upset. Agata comforted me saying that she has been to many of the places on our itinerary and she thinks the time we've allowed is fine for what we're aiming to do. If we wanted to see each place thoroughly a week per place would be needed, and that just isn't possible.

Our fourth conversation of the week occurred on Saturday morning after which we had reached a level of mutual understanding, and there were no hard feelings either way. Grandma was, and is, doing all she can to help – investigating ferries and trains, for example. I think it was fortunate the way it happened because she actually phoned on Friday evening – the night I was at Park – and she spoke to Agata. Agata told her that I had been upset after our conversation the night before. This gave her time to think about it before ringing to resolve the matter on Saturday morning. So now everything is fine and dandy, but in the space of thirty-six hours, I had gone from relief to stress to elation to despair to a plateau of dullness followed by a plateau of content.

On Sunday morning I went to an evangelical service run by an American Pastor. Terry had been a few times and told me about it. It was quite interesting. It takes place in a first-floor room in a nondescript building in a hidden-away part of Warsaw near Plac Bankowy. I enjoyed the singing and the friendly atmosphere, yet I still have some suspicion – some doubt – about this style of religion. The style of praying is certainly too over-the-top for me, but I agreed with the message put forth in the sermon – that one should be changed by going to church – that the purpose of church is to take something from it which you can apply to your daily living – that we should give joyfully

29

and not get overweight with religion, keeping it all to ourselves. This ties in very well with our religion lesson of today where the priest was talking about the word of God being our food of life and just as diets can be dangerous – neglecting God can also mean we don't have the energy for life. He was looking at the same issue but from another end of the scale. So what I learned from this is that there is a need for a balance between the two.

Meanwhile, I want to continue to sample all that Warsaw has to offer in terms of styles of worship as I search for what provides me with my desired balance between music and prayer, old and new symbols and simplicity, arousal and serenity. My desire to do something for the good of humankind in the name of God gets stronger every day, and I pray that God may reveal to me soon what my calling is. I feel it must be something physical and something personal, not connected with money.

After this, I intended to send a batch of emails, but due to a communication problem between Poland and America, I could not access my email account, so I went home. I tried again at the internet café, but this time the problem was that the only computer with an A-drive was reserved for an hour – I reserved it for the following day and left. I have now discovered that my school has Internet access which I will be able to use for free.

I had my first experience of a problem with a ticket monitor yesterday. I was with Pieter on the way to the studio, and we were travelling by metro. I had purchased two weekly tickets rather than a monthly ticket since I will be leaving on the 15th, but I didn't realise that with weekly tickets you have to punch holes in them like the ordinary day tickets. I tried to play the foreigner trick, but he ordered us off the train at the next stop. I was thoroughly amused and had no idea what the problem was. Pieter couldn't think how to explain and was feeling very guilty. I had to pay 49 złoty, 20 of which had to be borrowed from Pieter. I was laughing inside, but for Pieter's sake, I kept a straight face.

So, *wszystko albo nic*. I'm putting my all into this exchange. This afternoon I took a stroll on the site of the apartment blocks where Agnieszka lives. I allowed myself to observe and get a feel for the place. And this evening I can appreciate better what it feels like to be a young person in Poland as I went with Agnieszka to her evening tutoring in English. There is a class of 6 taught by a 23-year-old male Australian from Sydney who has been in Poland a shorter time than I have. Extra lessons after school are very common in Poland, particularly in languages. I have been contemplating getting some work teaching English, and this evening was an opportunity to see how it works and what it would be like. I have decided I'd rather not, as it is very time consuming, and I have no experience in dealing with tutoring 6 people at once. I would rather help my class for free than spend my time teaching others for money.

Agnieszka told me this evening that she is surprised but very pleased that I'm still attending school, even though I get bored in some of the lessons. She wondered how long it would be before I began to skip class and is very proud of my persistence. I was very glad when she said this and hope that the others in the class feel the same way because I am sure this is how I will keep friends. Irregular attendance is where the other exchange students went wrong and as a result, had a bad experience of school. Being a visitor comes with its privileges such as being invited to the *studniowka*, going on class excursions and using the internet for free, but you have to be prepared to live like a Polish student to be accepted by them.

4-3-98

Wednesdays – they're not good for me. Things go wrong, or I'm in a weird mood or something on Wednesday. My first experience of being lost, I remember, was a Wednesday, and it was last Wednesday when I was stressed about travel plans. Anyway, today was one of those moody days. Plus, when I finally found British Airways, they were closed.

The Rotary meeting was pretty lively tonight. Jake, of course, was absent but everyone else was there as it was payday. So there was Polish, English and Portuguese, plus a bit of Hungarian flying here, there and everywhere, and I'm feeling rather drained by it all. I feel rather embarrassed and inadequate when I think about the Brazilian exchange students who not only know their native Portuguese and the language of their host country, but also are fluent in English. It is very admirable. It's very difficult to describe how I feel – the word arrogant springs to mind, but I'm referring to the arrogance of the English language. I feel like I want to apologise for the fact that English is becoming the universal language – it's weird.

6-3-98

Now where was I? A friend rang and I never resumed writing yesterday. I began to write about my first Polish dancing lesson. Marlena from my class has been in this group – Promni – for about a year and her father is the Director. I went with them last night to the Agricultural University Hall where the rehearsals take place. The evening began with voice warm-up exercises because not only do they dance, but they sing as well. Then we changed – I was the only girl without a skirt to dance in, but it didn't matter. There were about sixty people there, and I was impressed to see an almost equal number of boys and girls. Most of them are university students. We started to learn a dance called *Mazura* which has some rather difficult steps. After this I went with the Beginners group to another room where we learnt the steps of the *Krakówa*. At the end we returned to the main hall to watch the more advanced group perform (sing and dance with instrumental accompaniment) a dance from a town in the mountains. *Było fantastycznie* [It was fantastic]. I enjoyed it, and they were keen for me to keep going, so I think it will become a regular Thursday evening commitment.

It was weird – as I was walking home from school today it occurred to me that I don't see my school friends as Polish any more. It's very difficult to describe, but perhaps I could say that I feel like one of them.

Our last period on a Friday is W.F, for which we take a change of clothes and trainers. We also must change shoes upon arrival and departure from school, so we need three pairs of shoes altogether. After W.F we changed from our gym shoes to our school shoes in the gym change room, only to go downstairs and change from our school shoes to our outside boots. It can get rather frustrating.

Yesterday in the Polish lesson I was passing notes (in Polish) with several people at once. It was quite fun. What is funnier is that the teacher can't shout at me because firstly she knows I probably wouldn't understand what she was saying and secondly, I am considered a guest.

I was very surprised and happy to wake up this morning and find that it had snowed overnight. I couldn't believe it, especially when juxtaposed with last evening's conversation with Marlena. We were discussing weather – how hot it is in Australia etc. etc. I said that I liked it when it snowed a few weeks ago in Warsaw, and it looks like snow has gone for good now until next winter.

Marlena's reply was, 'Anything can happen', but I secretly doubted that it would snow again. She was right. I went out early this morning into the back garden and wrote a big *DZIeN DOBry* [good morning] in the snow with footprints. I wanted to go back upstairs to see what it looked like from my bedroom, but I had to go to school, and by the time I got out of school all the snow had disappeared. I don't believe it, I just looked out the window, and it's snowing! It's like one of those snow shaker thingies in reverse – I'm on the inside, and the snow is on the outside.

8-3-98

It's great to be in an environment where girls can kiss each other on the cheek, and boys can dance without being accused of being homosexual. It's also fantastic to experience being among people who are proud of their nationality. By this I mean they are not ashamed to be Poles – I don't mean that they have a superiority complex like Americans. I think I've sussed the Polish character to be one of inner strength, and on the outside, they are relaxed and fun-loving.

Last night I went to a party. It's become a family joke – every time I go out Agata says, 'Another *impreza* [party]?' Anyway, it was at the house of Paweł (or Lamb, which is his nickname – I keep telling them that you don't pronounce the 'b'). He lives just around the corner near Lelewel. It was great – there were about fifteen people there, some who I'd already met and some new people. I felt very much at ease and happy in their company. We talked, listened to music, munched, drank, and danced a little. I particularly enjoyed talking to Michał's girlfriend Marija who spent eight years in the USA, so is fluent in both languages and has a job as a translator. Michał dotes on her, and they intend to get married next year.

We had an interesting conversation about racism based on Marija's experience in the USA. She was very much looked down upon for being Polish, and she said that having experienced being discriminated against has made her very tolerant and accepting. This made me think of the Aborigines and particularly the song 'Proud to Be'. Aborigines have every reason to hate white people, yet the majority look to the future with optimism and as the song says, 'We've got to unite' and 'live in harmony'.

My other events of yesterday include going with one school friend, Adela, to her photography lesson at the Palace of Culture, seeing *Titanic* with two school friends Katryna and Madlen, and Madlen's sister, and then visiting the internet café. While at the Palace of Culture, I enquired about some drawing lessons. It was quite a challenge trying to explain myself to the lady at the information desk, who thought I was merely a tourist who wanted to go up the tower. In the end, she called for a translator. It was rather embarrassing.

I went to check my email – five new messages. I was very excited. I love the atmosphere of that café – great music, nice people and interesting interior design. Having tried (and failed) to use the school computer to send and receive my emails, I don't think it's going to be a valid option, firstly because the computer is so slow and secondly, because I like going to the Internet café even though I have to pay each time.

9-3-98

I commented to Mum before I left Australia that I wanted to see how I would react when confronted by a variety of different situations. I think I can now say that I am happy with the way I've got out of 'holes', made decisions, organised things, and (as is true

35

to my character) tried to keep a balance. Yes, balance and variety are two very important words when it comes to defining me.

It has been a very freeing experience. Not that I didn't enjoy a very free childhood – I did – but what I am referring to is the intangible, unspoken-of chains that tie you down within your community and prescribe how you should act. I was contemplating this today and thinking back to how I used to act at church, at school, at home in Australia. The quote from *Maestro* popped into my head:

> 'once we begin to sense our childhoods,
> we are no longer children.'

It was only just the other day that I wrote on the back of my sheet of Polish verbs:

> 'Ornamental façades. Hiding the hypocrisy within.'
> [Peter Goldsworthy, *Maestro*]

This was about the experience of school in Poland. As I wrote in my article, the best thing about Lelewel is the warm, happy, friendly atmosphere but as I have learnt since, this is the 'ornamental façade' hiding the hypocrisy of immense stress and strict, demanding teachers. Agata told me some stories of the upsetting experiences Miranda and Alojzy had with teachers who wield their power unfairly. I am beginning to notice this at school – piles of homework, marks according to whether the teacher likes the student or not, neglecting to give help then shouting when a student gets it wrong. I think many of them envy me as I don't have to do the work, but they're still puzzled as to why I keep coming back to sit through their boring lessons. But I like them very much, and I just about know everyone's name now. There is one girl who scares me as she is fairly big but other than that she makes me feel so tiny when I speak to her. Agnieszka said she doesn't know why she doesn't want to speak to me because her English is very good.

Polish is beginning to be no longer a game. I get the sense that people are feeling I should be communicating seriously in Polish now. I'm trying very hard, and it's rather tiring. I find that certain people are very easy to understand – such as Martyna (I like her very much) and others, even though they are speaking the same language, are very difficult to understand – for instance, our homeroom teacher. Today I went to tell her that I will be absent for the next three weeks as I'm going on a trip (which I managed in Polish). She took the opportunity to sit me at the front of the class and fire questions at me. She asked if someone would translate for her, but I butted in and asked her to speak in Polish but slowly. I don't know what it was, but she is rather difficult to understand, so I was picking up a couple of words in each sentence and guessing the rest. Bad mistake. I answered 'no' to a question I thought was, 'Is politics popular in Australia?' but which I found out later was, 'Can you name any Australian politicians?' Tomorrow I will try and explain the misunderstanding and tell her that yes, I do know some Australian politicians!

After my busy Saturday, Sunday was fairly quiet and lazy. When it stopped raining I went for a walk in the nearby forest. It was like a mini vacation. The fun part was going alone because then I felt like I was exploring rather than being guided. I found peace among the trees, and as I came out of the forest it was interesting to hear the whoosh of the traffic gradually increase and see the tall, grey apartment blocks slowly materialise beyond the trees.

This evening I bought my plane ticket to London and gripped it in my cold hand all the way home. On the way I visited Agnieszka (who had been absent from school today) and bumped into Grigor from my class, who was returning from visiting her. Dora, also from my class, dropped by to return a book. That's the great thing about apartment blocks, it's easy just to go and visit someone, and you often see someone you know. I stayed for a while, and we chatted about school, travel etc. I corrected some English work for her sister. Agnieszka appreciated my visit. The reason she had been absent from school was that yesterday she spilt boiling water on her stomach which was now red and blistered.

It's weird, when I'm reading, each time I come across a new word I find myself sounding it out as if it's a Polish word. I've got into the habit now of reading with the Polish pronunciation in mind.

13-3-98

Two more sleeps. I'm going to document the trip in point form in my little trip book and expand upon this when I return. I said goodbye to my friends at school today and was very touched when my closest friends (Agnieszka, Danuta, Katryna, Mina) kissed me on the cheek and wished me all the best. (Marcel gave me £1.50 for packets of Big Red chewing gum.)

You know, I think I'm not so much changing but rather finding out what makes me as a person, grasping onto these threads and taking them further. One of the things I'm often doing is recapping past events and how they fell into place and thinking how incredibly lucky I am. And it is often the way that bad things turn out to be good and purposeful. I'm a strong believer in 'there is nothing either good or bad but thinking makes it so'

[Shakespeare, *Hamlet*]. I said this to Agata the other day as she was very stressed over a tax notice she'd received.

I have the reputation within the circle of exchange students of the girl who is doing everything and going everywhere. I'm very happy about this because I am not one to sit around and waste a year, particularly when there are so many opportunities just waiting to be grasped.

Today Agnieszka invited me to go with her and her family to the Baltic Sea for two weeks in August. She is just sooo nice.

I went to my second Promni rehearsal last night, this time with a skirt and better shoes. Again great fun. The singing was more extensive this time and sounded fabulous.

Yesterday I commented on a bead on Martyna's jumper, which turned out to be a key opening the door to a very interesting story. The bead was a part of some electrical device whose name in the Polish language is the same as 'opposition' and was worn as a symbol by those who began the uprising against communism in the early 1980's. Martyna's father was a messenger who climbed the Tatra Mountains at night to meet with the Slovakians and delivered papers outlining what needed to be done. It was after this that a protest was staged which was not violent, yet many were arrested and imprisoned including Martyna's father. The jumper she wore was his.

14-3-98

Almost ready to go. Everything is laid out ready to pack – just waiting on my safari pants to dry so I can iron them and pack everything together.

England, Ireland, France and Spain – here I come.

Western Europe

A ZEST FOR THE WEST [email report to Rotary]

On the 15th of March I donned a backpack, armed with my *Rough Guide to Europe* book and joined the ever-increasing subculture of young people worldwide who cannot contain their desire to see the world. It was an amazing three weeks – full of so many different experiences and challenges and plenty of fun.

I went by plane to Heathrow where I was met by Pip (our friend from Bristol who stayed with us in Australia for three months last year), her boyfriend Simon, and Jake – my travelling companion. We had it easy for the first couple of days as Pip and Simon provided us with accommodation, meals and dedicated their time to showing us some of the sights of south-west England. Oxford was one of these. We took an open-top bus tour around the sandstone city steeped in university tradition and an air of academia. Stonehenge is another of the SE England highlights and is a truly mysterious place. You are unable to actually walk among the stones but your entry fee entitles you to an electronic guided tour handset which you listen to as you walk around the perimeter. It suggests various theories as to what this monument represents as well as the few archaeological facts that are known. Quite thought-provoking.

While Oxford is built around the university, the protagonist in Bath is of course the Roman Baths, from which the city took its name. Like Stonehenge, as you tour the baths you carry with you a handset which explains everything as you go. It must have been quite a place when it was being used for its original purpose. I tried to imagine it filled with Romans during the Roman era or monks during the medieval era or aristocracy during the Jane Austen era! These experiences were, strangely enough, also new for Pip and Simon but it is very true that you don't see the tourist attractions in your own area until you have visitors from abroad. Similarly, people I've met from other countries are amazed that I haven't been to Uluru.

On St. Patrick's Day we left for Ireland. The ferry trip took about three hours across a calm emerald sea and as we approached the Isle in the late afternoon it looked as though it was being blessed from heaven – the way the sunlight fell in shafts through the clouds. We got a coach to Waterford arriving at 8.30 pm, found a hostel and then headed out for St. Patrick's night celebrations. We couldn't find any traditional Irish music in this small town but we tried the beautiful creamy Guinness that Ireland is so famous for and enjoyed watching and listening to the Irish celebrating their national day. We even came across a shop which had in big letters above the window *T. PHELAN – TOBACCONIST.* I had to take a photo of this! I proudly used my Irish surname for all the hostel and ticket reservations while we were in Ireland! The next day we left early for Dublin but spent the best part of the day in tranquil Kilkenny (half way between Waterford and Dublin). The highlight of this town is its castle which has been almost fully restored, and guided tours are provided of the interior. It's impressive while not being overly grand, and in a perfect situation by the river, surrounded by green lawns punctuated with patches of daffodils. This became our picnic spot for lunch.

My longing for a session of traditional Irish music (with bodhran [Irish drum]) was satisfied in Dublin. Not only was there a four-piece band but also a troupe of four Irish dancers. They provide entertainment every night in Fitzsimons pub (admittedly primarily for the tourists) in the hip and happening Temple Bar area of Dublin. It was great. The sounds, the rhythms, the atmosphere, the energy pulled at something inside of me and I wanted to stay all night. In one of their breaks I asked the bodhran player if she could show me a few things. As it was very busy and noisy at that time, she said why don't I come tomorrow at 7 pm.

My bodhran lesson was a small but exciting part of an extremely action-packed day in Dublin. We were at Trinity College Library for opening time where we saw the famous Book of Kells which is housed there. This is the illuminated manuscript of the four gospels completed by Irish monks in c. 800 AD. Also housed here is the oldest harp in Ireland which is depicted in the Guinness logo. After this, we went to the national museum then walked through the park and along the main shopping street. Here we split – I went to the Guinness museum and Jake the writer's museum. Did you know that there are 10 million pints of Guinness brewed daily worldwide? (2.5 million of these in Ireland.) We reunited at the Jameson distillery where we learned how whisky – another important Irish alcoholic beverage – is made. We had a meal at Tosca's – a café owned by the brother of a U2 band member and then I went to choral evensong at Christ Church Cathedral. Then there was of course my bodhran lesson and some more time spent listening to the band and watching the dancers.

Next stop was my grandparents' house in Leeds. Mum and Dad were there having arrived a week ago. My dad's parents came for the day and we had a family meal together. We only had two nights in Leeds and then headed for France. We travelled in the impressive Eurostar through the Chunnel and arrived in Paris about 9 pm. As Jake had already spent four days in Paris, and I intend to go in summer, this was simply an overnight stop en route to Bordeaux. We left early next morning arriving in Bordeaux at 11 am. After offloading our backpacks at the hostel we got a train to Saint Émilion – a beautiful vineyard village 30 mins west of Bordeaux. The sun beat down as we wandered the cobbled streets, lazed by the church and contemplated the landscape from the top of the bell tower. The following day we leisurely explored the city of Bordeaux then caught the 7 pm train to Madrid (our first overnight train trip). We had to change at the border – a place called

Irun – which we thought was part of France but when we started to read the signs we realised we were in Spain. For a while it was a case of 'What country are we in?!' We had an hour in this town, and since we wanted to buy a drink, but had no currency for Spain, we had to find an ATM. We accomplished this successfully and consulted our 'Bible of travelling' for the exchange rate. I selected what I thought was an appropriate amount but when the machine spat out an abundance of notes I realised that I had misread where the decimal point was and had withdrawn the equivalent of $500 rather than $50! Luckily Jake had not yet withdrawn so we solved the problem by splitting money between us and keeping a tally of what we spent so that he would pay me back later in the trip.

We arrived in Madrid at 8.30 am and spent the day exploring on foot as per the walking tour outlined in the *Lonely Planet Guide*. Madrid has a huge central park, originally used as a retreat for royalty. In the centre is a lake headed by a large stone monument and amphitheatre where you can hire a boat. This is what we did as the sun was setting, serenaded by the sounds of a little band of Spanish musicians who were playing on the shore. Our second day in Madrid was spent mostly at the Reina Sofia art gallery. It was great to see the original *Guernica* by Picasso which I had studied in school. Not only was it protected by an alarmed barrier but there were two men constantly guarding it. This was also the day I was almost mugged. I left Jake's side for only a few minutes and a man came up to me and started pointing to something on my right shoulder and talking in Spanish. I thought he was just trying to tell me that I had something on my shoulder but I couldn't see anything. Then I felt a tug at my waist bag which I was wearing on my stomach. I turned around to find a second man in front of me and my waist bag open. By this time Jake had come over and the two men wandered off. I checked my wallet and was thankful to find that they hadn't had time to take anything. I was lucky. Nifty trick though – one distracts while the other steals.

From here the planned itinerary changed. We decided we wanted to go to Africa for a day which meant getting the overnight train from Madrid to the south coast and the ferry to Tangier in the morning. It wasn't quite as easy as this however. Once in Algeciras (where the ferry leaves from) we had to wait 3 hours for the next ferry, which then left 1 hour late. On arrival we, along with 4 Americans, were delayed because we hadn't had our passports stamped. It was late afternoon by the time we got off the ferry but there is no way I would take back the incredible experience that was to follow, despite the preliminary hassles. We were immediately greeted by a hoard of Arabic tourist men (or so they claimed). The way in which one of them (Larry) took us aside and started telling us (in English) how he could escort us to a lovely hotel and give us a tour of the city, followed by his questions as to where we were from and how long we were going to be there, was rather suspicious, not to mention the threats that if we didn't accept his services bad things could happen to us in the streets!

First of all we confirmed how much his services would cost, then decided to accept as long as he took us to the hotel we had chosen from my guide book. He did. It was a cheap but very nice place with mosaic walls and tropical courtyards. He waited outside while we got a room. The first place he took us was a carpet shop where we were taken upstairs and treated to mint tea and a show by one of the shopkeepers explaining the different carpets made in Morocco. It was very interesting but then came the catch. We were made to feel obliged to buy a carpet. They were such crafty salesmen – asked us which we liked best, split us up, asked us how much we would offer for it in our own currency (the conversion tables and calculator were at the ready) and they had a comeback for every excuse. I had trouble trying to explain that it was not the price that was too much but the fact that I have a dust allergy and couldn't have a carpet in my room anyway. He replied that the particular one I liked is no problem for allergies. As a last resort he tried the line that I could sell it in my home country and make a huge profit. Jake meanwhile was suffering similar pressure with the other shopkeeper, the difference being he was genuinely interested but wanted time to think about it away from this intense environment. But it seemed like they weren't going to let us go until we had made a deal. I almost shook hands with him for $100 just so we could get out of there but realised that that was part of their motive and I was determined not to succumb. Another angle they tried was that of pathos – that they need the money for their families and it's not much to us but to them it's a livelihood. I think this was closer to the truth than any of the others, but we finally got out of there saying we'd come back when we had thought about it.

We were really in need of some food so we asked Larry to take us to a restaurant where we had a traditional Moroccan meal of soup with flat bread and couscous and kebabs (accompanied by more mint tea). On our tour of the city Larry happened to take us past the carpet shop again and we almost became embroiled in yet another interrogation session. They told us they had stayed open in the hope that we would return, but no deal was made as Jake could not accept the amount they were offering. Larry showed us the market square and the Kasbah (Royal Palace) from which there is a great view of the beach. It was an amazing experience just to walk through the narrow streets thronging with people as the sounds from the mosque summoned them to prayer. There were women walking arm in arm completely covered apart from their faces, children playing with a ball in tiny spaces, men drinking in bars or selling things on the street. As we walked past a group of children, a small boy asked me:
'American?'
'No Australian' I replied.
'Welcome' he said.
It was so sweet.

We paid our guide and returned to the hotel. We were about to go to bed when there was a knock at the door. We were informed that there was someone to see us in the foyer. Yes, the carpet man actually came to our hotel, carpet under one arm with a final offer of US$80 which Jake couldn't resist. He even drove us to the ATM so that we could get the money to pay him! So everyone was happy in the end.

Getting out of Morocco was almost as difficult as getting in. Jake's alarm didn't go off. We awoke at 7.20 am. The ferry was at 7.30 am. That was the quickest we'd ever got out of a hotel room, and if the gates to the city hadn't been locked, forcing us to go around, we would have made it. But instead we had to wait for the 9.00 am ferry. This of course meant that we didn't make the connecting train to Granada. We got there eventually though and found some accommodation. It rained for our one day in Granada but it did not hinder too much our visit to the Magnificent Alhambra – the Arabic Palace and gardens that Granada is famous for. The plan was to leave that night on the overnight train to Barcelona but just as we were about to leave I became violently ill with travellers' curse – gastro. The culprit – most probably some Greek food we had the night before. So we ended up staying in Granada for another night and day. It was a harrowing experience but Jake did a good job of looking after me. I look at it as just another pearl on my string of experiences – if not so shiny as the others.

Our trip concluded with three days in Barcelona. We had a great hotel there – right near La Rambla ('the' street in Barcelona) – a tree-lined avenue, home to buskers, outdoor cafés and flower stalls. Also very handy was the huge market place – La Boqueria – our one-stop-shop for breakfast and lunch. We got huge delicious strawberries dirt cheap. One of the highlights of Barcelona was the architecture of Gaudi of which we saw two examples: Sagrada Familia, the massive unfinished church, and Parc Guell, the incredible inner-city palace. I love his ideas, his use of space and his balance between art and practicality. The colourful and energetic Flamenco show that we saw was another highlight. We, of course, saw the Olympic site, the beach (unfortunately not warm enough for swimming) and the Picasso Museum.

Due to our diversion to Africa, our extra day in Granada as a result of unforeseen circumstances, and our extra two days in Barcelona, we decided to shorten the end of the trip by skipping Geneva and going straight to Munich (a night and a day on the train). We intended to stay a night and a day in Munich, but when we arrived and discovered that there was a convention on and thus no accommodation under 200DM, we had no option but to get the train that night to Warsaw. In our three hours in Munich we did have time to check out the most famous of its beer halls where rows of Germans down the amber liquid to the sounds of Bavarian music played by a small group of musicians – quite a cultural experience. So, after a night, a day, a night and another day on the train, with breaks of inconvenient length, we arrived in Warsaw (where the first signs of spring are emerging), exhausted but with fond memories of an adventure that will not be forgotten in a hurry!

Żoliborz

I spent a lot of time during the trip agonising over the nature of our relationship – whether I liked Jake as more than a friend; what he thought of me, whether I should make a move or not... I can't really say it has been resolved either – well at least not openly, but now that I look back on the trip and the good times we had as friends I'm happy to keep it that way. We got on really well – no fights, plenty of laughter and teasing and silences weren't awkward. Jake is the first male friend I consider to be on the same level as my girlfriends. I love his ideas, perspectives, attitude, romantic nature, wit, sense of humour, sense of adventure, yet there was still this tension I felt as a result of not being sure of how we related to each other. His non-judgemental character and the contradictory signals I received made it difficult to determine what he thought of me.

For example, the time he read me a poem he had written about a girl who kissed him in Italy – was this a 'come on' or was it a warning against trying anything because he likes this girl – or was he simply bragging? And then there was the time when we were discussing when we could fit in a trip to Russia and he looked at me with imploring eyes and said 'But I think we should go together!' And then there were the many times his indignation showed that he thought I was immature e.g. wanting to play 20 questions.

From one of the conversations we had towards the end of the trip I basically determined that he doesn't like me as more than a friend. We were talking about what we look for in a lover. He said sense of humour, self-confidence, intelligence, maturity and of course that certain special something. He also said he most definitely goes for older women. Incidentally mine are sense of humour, sense of adventure, intelligence, that special something, preferably blonde hair and blue eyes (I don't know why), and I have to like myself when I'm around them. (I didn't say these last two out loud.) All of which Jake possesses except that special something.

For some reason I still desire this conclusion to be confirmed verbally. On so many occasions I almost asked him if he liked me as anything more than just a friend but lacked the courage. A small voice inside my head (probably influenced by Jake himself) tells me *Who cares what he thinks about you?* But I do care because now that I've decided he is a valuable friend I want confirmation that it's mutual because friendship is a two-way thing. I only ever heard him talk about one male friend – Oliver – yet he mentioned so many female friends. He's certainly a ladies' man and by becoming his friend it seems I'll be joining the merry band of female followers he seems to have, and I will try to be content with this role.

It was great to see my classmates again today. They were also pleased to see me and eager to hear about my adventures. I've been plunged back into the Polish language but thankfully it's quickly coming back to me. They liked my postcard which I noticed was sitting on our homeroom desk next to the Australian flag. Agnieszka told me it was quite funny because I had written that I sleep with Guinness instead of I drank Guinness. Marcel was melodramatically upset when I told him that Big Red is no longer produced and returned his £1.50.

Already the class is planning a second trip for the year – this time in September and probably to the coast, despite the fact that the majority voted for the mountains. Travel, travel and more travel – this is sooo cool.

I found myself looking at Warsaw with tourist's eyes again, like I was in my first few weeks here, but at the same time it feels like I've come home. It's a very weird feeling.

7-4-98

Mum often said I always like to pigeon-hole things – part of my organisation streak – but the one thing I can't pigeon-hole is myself. I've given a lot of time to observation and thought about where I fit in the scheme of things and searching for a model on which to base myself, particularly with regards to clothes. Am I a city sophisticate or a grunge type? Jake was no help. He wouldn't be serious when I asked him if he thought I fitted any particular stereotype. Whenever I turn to the subject of self-definition, he seems determined not to influence, which makes me more eager to know his opinion. Never-the-less I think fashion is another one of those things (like music) where I like a variety. For example this week I'm feeling comfortable in more sophisticated attire after three weeks of casual backpacker gear. But I have resolved to get rid of the clothes that I don't feel good in and take more notice of the 'feel-good' factor when purchasing clothes in the future. I think clothes do influence self-confidence and it's about time I took more care in choosing my own clothes rather than wearing a mish-mash of hand-me-downs, presents and clothes from ages ago.

I am really looking forward to meeting my host sister Miranda on Thursday. Agata came back this evening but Miranda will stay 2 more days and come to Warsaw by train on Thursday. It is likely that she will go again to Kraków for a couple of days next week and hopefully I'll be able to go with her. On Tuesday next week Agnieszka has invited me to go with her and her sister to Częstochowa, a town near Warsaw, for a special mass.

I went out on Alojzy's bike for an hour this afternoon. I'm having to get out of thinking of riding as my transport to get me from one place to another, and think of it simply as an enjoyable activity to do for exercise. I rode along the Vistula River past the Old Town. There were many people out enjoying the sunshine – riding, walking, fishing and of course plenty of couples canoodling. I'm glad I took the opportunity to go for a ride as the forecast is for rain tomorrow.

One thing Jake did allow me to learn about myself is that I'm a grey person. What I mean is best illustrated by the following example. When we were in Munich he said, 'Never a straight answer from you – nothing is ever black or white to you.' That's part of my balance streak – trying to find compromises that incorporate a bit of everything, which comes back to the variety idea. Do you sense that we're going around in circles? I do!

This reminds me of an anecdote from my travels. I really felt like a citizen of the world especially when I arrived in Heathrow, an Australian with a British passport who started to answer the English customs officer in Polish! I was telling Agata this evening about our incredible experience in Tangier. She was naturally very interested because she's been there. I was just thinking about it all again and remembered the instance where we had returned to our hotel and Jake made some comment about the amazing experience we were having. I said, 'Imagine it as a female, two years younger and...' What I wanted to say was ...*and just got your period!* The adrenaline was certainly pumping that evening – my eyes couldn't have been wider, my brain more alert (yet numb at the same time with all the activity), or my body more overworked, what with all the walking and carrying and the effect of the hormonal change. But as I wrote in my story of the trip, I wouldn't take back that experience; it was dumbfounding. And we were so naive about the place – knew virtually nothing of its people, customs, language, organisation. Had no idea what to expect. Well actually the image I had of it was totally contradictory to the real thing, i.e. open, hot, sandy, clean, flat, a few market stalls and camels. Take these words, change them to their opposites and you are half way to having an image of what it was really like.

8-4-98

At school today a couple of uni students came to give a psychological test to our class during a free lesson we had. It happened to be a page of adjectives (in Polish of course) and we had to circle the ones that applied to us. What a great resource for me! I kept it and am in the process of looking them all up in the dictionary. At first I went through all 300 and wrote the ones I knew and guessed at ones that sound like they're based on English ones.

In biology the teacher asked me to stand up and asked why I was smiling. The others tried to explain that I didn't understand Polish. She then started to rant and rave saying why do I come to these lessons if I don't understand them.

The last lesson was English and I talked to the class about my trip and showed them my photos. They were very grateful for this as they didn't have to do any work. The remainder of the lesson was taken up with discussing the Easter traditions in Poland compared with those in Australia. So now I know what to expect this weekend and it sounds great – lots of cakes!

I wrote some more letters at school today but I'm having trouble finding a computer and printer so I can print the *Zest for the West* chronicle which I want to include with the letters. The printer at school has no ink cartridge and the computer downstairs is not compatible with Windows 95.

I always come home from Rotary meetings dissatisfied – this time not as much as some other previous meetings, but I can say that they are certainly not uplifting. My counsellor complained about how busy he is and asked me to investigate Polish lessons for myself. I'm only annoyed I didn't take the initiative myself earlier. Karol the architect wasn't there. I was pleased however that Jake reacted the same as I did when seeing my photos of the trip. I could see the fond memories being reawoken inside of him. Photos tend to define the blur – or at least that's what I've found. The danger comes when they begin to redefine it.

11-4-98

It's nice to go to the shops, or the city, or simply to the bus stop and see people I know from school. This is exactly the type of thing I would desperately avoid when I was younger. I used to think school was the place to see people from school and nowhere else. If I saw someone I knew in the street I would avoid eye contact and try to go unnoticed. Strange when I look back on it now.

Miranda is finally here. She arrived last night by train from Kraków. She is really nice, insists on speaking with me in Polish and is a lot like her mother. I was very much looking forward to meeting her – as I said to Agata at the station – 'I've never had a sister before.' We are making plans to go to Kraków together next week!

The last two days I've spent helping Agata with the preparations for Easter. I made a carrot cake and helped Agata make a traditional Polish Easter cake. I've been into the city both days also; on Thursday to investigate Polish lessons at the uni (I start after Easter – two evenings a week) and on Friday to get mum an amber necklace, and the family some Easter gifts. I unexpectedly spent quite a while in the American book shop where I bought a book about Polish traditions and recipes, and a book of Polish legends. I would have liked to do some egg painting for Easter which is described in the first book, but we don't have the materials for it. Agata showed me one that Judyta made for her in 1995.

It is now Saturday morning – the Easter weekend ahead of me which promises to be culturally very interesting, gastronomically very satisfying and religiously very solemn.

13-4-98

I had my first twinges of homesickness today brought on by one of Agata and Walenty's very vocal arguments, which reminded me of the troubled times in my family during 1996. But a Guinness in the Irish Pub, surrounded by the company of Miranda and co. soon put an end to it. I decided not to deny it and to realise that it would pass.

Yes, the Easter weekend was all that it promised to be. On Saturday morning Miranda and I decorated six eggs – not in the traditional way with wax, but with coloured pens instead. I really enjoyed this as I was feeling like I needed a bit of a creative outlet. Agata prepared the baskets of bread, sausage, salt, pepper, orange, decorated with greenery, to which we added the coloured eggs. We then drove to the Old Town to have them blessed by the priest in one of the churches. There were so many people there doing the same. We then met my host uncle and family with whom we walked from church to church to observe the displays of Christ's grave. We returned home for a huge *obiad* shared with Judyta, Janiusz and their son Mandek.

On Sunday Miranda and I met two Spanish friends of hers at the railway station. They study in Helsinki with her and were in Warsaw for a day, so Miranda said she would help them find accommodation and show them around a bit. Accommodation sorted, we went to the Old Town via Warsaw University and the Tomb of the Unknown Soldier. We left them at about 2.30 pm, returning home for *obiad*. The weather was cool but dry and sunny – not like today which is cold and wet – it even started to snow on our way back from the pub this evening.

It's 12.10 am now and I have to get up to go to Częstochowa in five hours – ahhh…

14-4-98

While we were at the house of Janiusz and Judyta yesterday, the adults were talking about their children, me included. They were saying that whenever their children are home or with them, all responsibility for organisation is offloaded onto the parents. In other words we take advantage of the opportunity to rely on someone else to do everything for us, yet when we are away from home (Miranda in Helsinki, Alojzy in Australia or me travelling around Europe) we are forced into doing things for ourselves and we prove that it is possible – we can be responsible and organised. I think this is very true, but it means that our parents never really see us in our true state, which I think is rather sad and perhaps the reason I'm so keen to tell my parents about all my experiences and feelings. Plus it's the first time we have really corresponded because, of course, there is no need for long letters when you're living with one another. I see them now as best friends rather than parents, knowing that we can love each other at a distance. I know I'm a person who needs to be loved and I have plenty of love to give.

My feelings for Agnieszka come close to the love of friendship, but yet I've only known her for not quite three months. I spent the day with her and her sister today in Częstochowa. It was an early start and a rough journey (travelling in the corridor of an old slow train for three hours). It was the special Mass for *Matura* [final year of high school] students from Warsaw so that's why the train was packed. Once we got there we stood and waited for 1½ hours (the priest got caught in traffic between Warsaw and Częstochowa) and then for another 1½ hours through the service. I enjoyed the music although it was not brilliant quality. I could recognise the parts of the Mass much more clearly than previously by concentrating on what was being said. It was very tiring but a very interesting cultural experience. We had a bit of free time afterwards so I bought a necklace and some hair clips from the street markets and we got hamburgers in a café. We had to run for the train which was again just as full as the one on the way there, but this time we managed to squeeze into one of the compartments and sat five in a space for four. I am now very, very tired.

15-4-98

Whoops! I stuffed up. Got in trouble tonight. Not only did I get home late but I hadn't locked the door when I left! I really regret it and am deeply sorry but it was difficult apologising to Agata when she had a smirk on her face, even though I know she was very serious inside. And guess what? It's a Wednesday!! I told you things always go wrong on Wednesday.

The reason I was late was because I went to the internet café after the Rotary meeting and you know how that just changes the concept of time in some weird way – consumes it, squishes it and spits it back out suddenly to shock and surprise you. Anyway, in reading an email from Ron [Australian District Rotarian] I've discovered another stuff up I've made – not only mentioning the Guinness in Dublin but also the note I sent to the Rotary club saying they can expect my story from Ron, when in fact they can't as he said he would only show it to select members due to some people's opinions of youth exchange students travelling. I'm very pleased with Ron's understanding approach and his encouragement to continue communicating with him about anything and everything, plus his agreement for reports to be electronic from now on. I remember back to the time when I was uncomfortable in his presence and found it difficult to talk to him, whereas now, at a distance, communicating in writing is great!

Writing is something I'm doing a lot of. Emails, letters, articles for the school magazine and of course diary entries. This is likely to increase since I'm starting Polish lessons next week which will inevitably involve homework.

Since I've come back I've had this sudden desire for knowledge through reading, music and videos – I want to learn about countries, their history, their people, current events and architecture. Hence I've bought books on Poland, become a member at the British Council which has a library of English books and videos, and I'm starting to buy magazines (not the crap glam stuff but *TIME*). I think this is a result of the lack of reading matter I took on the trip. I left my novel behind thinking I wouldn't have time for reading, and if I did, I should read about the country I was in from my *Lonely Planet* book, but really I should be making the most of every minute I had in a place. I now see the fault in that and, as Jake said, something you read might give you a new insight into where you are without actually being about that specific place. He added, in contradiction to my notion that it is wasting valuable time, that sometimes escape through 'art' is a necessary refresher. This reminds me of Keats!

So I think I'm keeping a balance between absorbing knowledge and experience through reading/watching/doing and reciprocating in the form of writing and giving. This is the essence of an 'exchange' I suppose. I have to remember that it's not all me, me, me, but what I can do for others as well. Spending some time with Jake and Terry in a pub this evening between the meeting and the internet café (I didn't tell Agata that bit) was a stark reminder of this. I could use Shakespeare's sponge metaphor in Hamlet to describe Jake. He listens, he watches, he learns, he absorbs yet gives very little indication of his feelings, thoughts, ideas or experiences unless asked, and only sometimes will give an extended response. For example, Terry and I both talked about our family lives, both in Poland and at home, yet we learnt nothing of his.

The Rotary meeting wasn't too bad. There was only Jake, Terry and me of the exchange students there. The formal part was over in an hour. I have an arrangement with Karol the architect for next week. I have the 513 zł for my Polish lessons. One thing I feel when I go to Rotary meetings is the necessity to boast to the other exchange students about what I've been doing, and all the friends I've made, to try and prove that I'm having a better exchange than them. It sounds terrible when put like this and I really don't like feeling this way. Perhaps it's not so much one-upmanship as my personal need to tell someone 'all about it' as I used to with Mum. Since Agata is often too busy for me, or responds indifferently when I tell her about my experiences, I seek a listener in another exchange student – usually Jake – and since he is all ears and not much mouth I tend to feel like it's me, me, me all the time, and hence the feeling that I am boasting.

Meanwhile I hope that my email friends who receive all my stories don't think I'm boasting. Looking back on the trip now it doesn't seem like such a big deal, because once in Europe, travelling around it, crossing boundaries is commonplace, but when I think about it from an Australian point of view, just as I did when receiving Fiona's letters from Poland last year, it seems so exotic. My friends say they are terribly envious. I just hope this doesn't put a rift in these friendships. They keep writing so that's a good sign.

It's 1 am. I'm getting very little sleep lately and drinking coffee and coke. It's terribly unhealthy.

16-4-98

We had a very thought-provoking conversation in English today which when juxtaposed with yesterday's diary entry is quite interesting. The stimulus was two articles about a father/daughter relationship, one from the daughter's perspective, the other from the father's perspective. From this theme of the generation gap developed a conversation about bringing up children and who is responsible when a child goes off the rails – are they born like that or is it the way they've been brought up? Is it the child's fault, the parents' fault or the fault of mass media, school etc. which all contribute to a child's character? Our teacher was trying to convince us that it is the parents' fault, saying that whenever a child goes off the rails there is usually something wrong at home. I'm not convinced. On the other hand, as Olga pointed out, there isn't a family who doesn't have problems, and these problems are usually due to lack of communication, which is vital, as communication with peers is often not as satisfying. This reminded me of what I wrote last night about the need to talk about my experiences, and feeling not quite right in doing this with other exchange students due to the fact that I feel like I'm bragging when I do.

The conversation moved from here to considering how we would bring up our own children – like our parents brought us up, or with greater freedom? This brought us back to the task of pointing the finger at who's to blame for a child's actions which we concluded depends on the amount of freedom the child is given by his/her parents i.e. the more freedom, the greater responsibility for his/her own actions (here we were of course discussing adolescents rather than small children). This led me to think of the freedom we enjoy as exchange students here in Poland, which Jake and I have often commented on. In comparison to other host countries, we can be very grateful for the ease with which we can go on trips. What I wrote about Agata – being indifferent in her responses to my stories, is not true – of course she is very interested and attentive. I bought them a pot plant today in apology for last night and it brought tears to Agata's eyes. She hugged me and told me she liked me very much and she hadn't meant to shout. But it wasn't that – I had deserved it – I genuinely wanted to apologise for leaving the door unlocked and not phoning to say what time I'd be home.

19-4-98

'Life will never be the same
Life is changing.'

The words of a song on the radio as we drove to the house of Judyta and Janiusz this afternoon, and words that are certainly true of my life at present. As I wrote in my letter to my Australian friend Philippa this weekend, some of the changes I've noticed so far include greater independence and the love of that freedom, drinking tea, coffee and alcohol, greater confidence, I don't let small things bother me, I'm better at coping with change and more flexible and, finally, I can't stand not having a plan in place for the following day, if not the week.

I commented on the painting Judyta and Janiusz have on the wall of their dining room – a scene from the Old Town, and Janiusz told me the artist lived downstairs. He arranged for me to go and see some more of his paintings in his apartment. He paints landscapes in oils and watercolours, usually of Warsaw and flowers. I really liked them but the one Judyta and Janiusz have remains my favourite. In my ideal house (which is slowly coming together in my head) I would have it on my bedroom wall at the foot of my large pinewood bed (one of those old-fashioned ones with the roof thingy) so I'd see it each morning when I awoke and remember my wonderful year in Warsaw. Three months I've been here now.

Not only does demand exceed supply with movie tickets in Warsaw but also with cars, I have discovered. Mandek was explaining to me that every month a group of people make a payment of a certain amount to this intermediary company, and each month one person in the group gets a car, and another car is given to the person in the group who makes the highest offer. Gradually, one by one, everyone in the group gets a car – the last person after about three years. Apparently it is a system that was invented in Argentina. Very interesting.

Yesterday as Agata was busy filling out documents, I made *obiad*, after which I went to Plac Wilsona and bought tickets for the 5.15 pm screening of *Siedem lat w Tibecie* (Seven Years in Tibet). I really enjoyed the film. It was full of interesting historical juxtapositions. I love juxtapositions. As the two weary Austrian travellers entered Tibet's holy city with no knowledge of its customs it reminded me so much of Jake and me in Tangier! And after the beautiful scenery of the Himalayas I want to go climbing there. One day I will. I could sympathise with the little Dalai Lama in his desire to learn about the world. If I attain my father's knowledge and my mother's wisdom I'll be happy.

22-4-98

I think Wednesday happened on Monday this week. Yes, it was Monday when everything went wrong. I used the internet at school but only had time to read my emails as by 9.30 am it got too slow. The last two lessons of the day were substituted with two more Polish lessons making a total of four Polish lessons in one day. *No way* I thought, so I went home. I composed some emails onto disk then headed into the city. Couldn't pay for my Polish lessons as the uni office was closed, couldn't use the uni computers as they were all taken, as were those at the internet café, had to wait 15 minutes at the post office just to get stamps for two letters, couldn't return my video and borrow another as the British Council library is closed on Mondays, went back to the internet café and finally got emailing. There was one from Kylie in Budapest to say that, *yes*, she'd love to travel with me. It's so exciting.

Tuesday was interesting. I had an appointment to meet Karol the architect at the Warsaw School of Architecture at 12.30 pm. It's a large old building in the centre of the city dedicated to producing architects. Everything happens at the one site – drawing on the top floor, modelling on the second, lectures on the first and history and library at ground level. In the basement is a shop selling everything an architecture student would want, plus the student club catering to the needs of sustenance and socialisation. There's even a courtyard of sculptures where students can sit during the warmer months. The demand for the course here is high but the demand for architects in the workforce is low. The course is only four years plus another half year for a diploma, and I was surprised to discover that they don't have work experience. From the shop I bought a pad, two pencils and a case to keep them in, and then in the café I was given my first draughting lesson. This afternoon I practiced the skills Karol showed me, only to be shot down in flames when I produced my drawings at the meeting tonight. It was, however, constructive criticism and very useful. I think I am mature enough to realise this now, rather than take it to heart as I would have done (and did) a few years ago. So I have quite a bit of practice to do and nine months in which to do it. I'm glad I'm making these mistakes now and not half-way through first year architecture at uni.

Last night was my first formal Polish lesson. It's a class of 14 representing 12 different countries. I'm the youngest and have come the furthest. I found it easy but useful as it's a more formal type of Polish that we are learning, rather than the colloquial I've picked up from listening.

After the Rotary meeting, like last week, Terry, Jake and I went to a pub. It was a weird experience. Terry talked non-stop about feeling depressed about going home. I was caught between wanting to help (but I didn't know whether he just wanted to be listened to or whether he wanted us to provide the answers) and dismissing him as an idiot (as Jake was doing by his obvious gestures of discomfort at being there). I'm still totally mixed up about how I feel about Jake, or moreover what he thinks of me. Just the other day I wrote in my letter to Philippa that he's everything I'd look for in a lifelong companion except for the fact that I'd have to be certain the feeling was mutual. But now it's very easy to think of him as just the person I travelled around Europe with. For one thing I don't feel comfortable with him because I don't like myself when I'm around him, and that is because, although it's probably not intended, I feel like I'm being seen in a condescending manner. This makes me self-conscious about what I say and do and hence uncomfortable. And then there's the question of religion and Jake's lack of belief in anything. This was quite a hot topic tonight in the pub. Terry gave quite a sermon on his views of religion, church and Christianity with strong suggestions that he hoped Jake would turn to Christianity. Although Jake was eager to leave, he did say the conversation would be continued at a later date – just a ploy to get out or a chance for him to gather his thoughts on the topic? Maybe neither! It's so hard to tell with him, we're not on the same wavelength. This was evident on our travels, when I come to think of it: the number of misunderstandings we had because I didn't get where he was coming from or simply couldn't understand his accent. Now that I look at it, liking myself in their presence, some religious belief and a similar wavelength are three characteristics I'd class as vital in a lifelong companion. So as you can see I'm still mixed up about Jake. I don't know why I bother worrying as he'll be gone in 2½ months.

23-4-98

Agata tells me I'm like Alojzy and Miranda in that I can't stay too long in one place. There's my variety characteristic rearing its head again. I think, though, I can stay in one place for a while as long as I'm keeping busy with a variety of different activities and I'm certainly doing that.

The weather was beautiful today. For the first time we spent the break times outside in the courtyard lying on the grass, basking in the sunshine. When I got home I went out on the balcony in shorts, T-shirt and sunglasses to finish my letter to Mum and Dad and grandparents. There really is a change in the general personality of the population with the change in weather.

24-4-98

One of the positive aspects of most people living in apartment blocks is that there is more room for green open spaces and forests for recreational purposes. I made use of these today as after school I went out on the bike for an hour or so. I felt like a child again as I rode down budded avenues and along leafy forest trails unconstrained as to which way to go – exploring a European forest with the same carefreeness as I explored the Australian bush as a child.

This evening I went to see *Good Will Hunting*. Brilliant movie. Very thought-provoking, and to think it was written by two 17-year-olds. The strong message I got out of it was that we must use the gifts we have for the good of others if not for ourselves. I thought it had quite a strong correlation with the parable of the Talents. The psychological insight was exquisite and it was very well acted by all. I wish I was like Minnie Driver's character – I aspire to having that kind of confidence and matter of fact nature. And I love the pun of the title. I can definitely understand why Jake liked it so much. There we go again – mentioning Jake – he seems to be in almost every diary entry lately. I've been thinking about how strange our contact has been since we've returned to Warsaw – it's as if once we're no longer in the travelling situation, where we were comfortable with the idea of being travelling companions, we don't know how to relate to one another as friends and fellow exchange students. I think it would be correct to say that our friendship climaxed in Granada – until then it was developing and after this, as we were heading for home, we became a little less tolerant and more unsure of one another.

I think I gave out the wrong signals tonight by dressing nicely to go to the movies with Pieter. Agata gave me a 'knowing look' but if she suspects something she's wrong. It reminded me of when I was showing Walenty the photos of the trip, and he came to the one of Jake eating pizza in bed. From the photo it was unclear that there were two separate beds and Walenty asked me something like 'You slept in a separate bed didn't you?' The irony is that the most passionate I've ever got with a guy happened under his very roof and was with neither of these guys!

25-4-98

It was an absolutely beautiful day weather-wise today. First thing, Agata and I went to the Russian markets on the other side of the Vistula River. Fascinating place. So many people and so many stalls selling all sorts of things really cheap. I bought eight CDs and a cardigan. The CDs are pirated of course, but you can get five for the price of one in a shop. I had arranged to meet Martyna and off we went together on bikes into the beautiful spring day. We rode to Łazienki Palace via the Wisła Strada where the cycle track was partly flooded due to the high level of the river. It is water from the south of Poland whose escape to the ocean is along the Vistula and hence via Warsaw. Łazienki in spring is beautiful. The last time I was there was for the Annie Leibowitz exhibition when everywhere was covered in thick snow. It was beautiful then and it's beautiful now. I didn't see the 'Palace on the water' the first time so this was lovely.

We bought ice-creams and sat eating them by the Palace, sun shining, people milling around and a peacock calling loudly from his perch in a nearby tree. In our jaunt around the park we saw a scampering squirrel. The last time I saw a squirrel would have been Roundhay Park in England in 1991.

Martyna is great company – we talked about all sorts of things and had some good laughs. Out of all the people in our class I think I feel the most comfortable with her. She's invited me to go camping and climbing with her on the Labour Day holiday at the beginning of May, which I'd love to do, only I'm committed to the Promni concert on the 2nd. Perhaps I can go by train after the concert and meet them there. It's a place between Kraków and Częstochowa.

27-4-98

Sunday was just as fun and varied as Saturday. In the morning I went to visit Agnieszka but upon learning she was at church decided to go to the service also. The congregation was spilling out into the courtyard and the music group were playing. Afterwards I walked back with Agnieszka and her sister and we arranged to meet that afternoon at Łazienki for the concert in Agrykola.

After this I went and met Terry at his church and asked him if he wanted to come with me to the Promni rehearsal and afterwards the concert in the park. He agreed. Unfortunately my group was on their break when we arrived at the hall, but we got to see the older group and the children dance. I think Terry was impressed – as much with what he saw as with how many people I knew and spoke Polish with. I find the voice in my head asking, *There, are you satisfied that you have now bragged to another exchange student?* And the other voice answering

No, really, I asked Terry along because I knew he'd been feeling depressed and didn't have any money. This was something free and different for him.

Anyway, we stayed for an hour then caught the bus to Agrykola. Earlier in the day I spotted Pieter on Krakówskie Przedmiescie. He too was going to the concert so we arranged to meet there at 3.30 pm – I suggested near the bus stop at the top of the hill, but agreed with his suggestion of the music control panel in front of the stage. There were so many people that this was impossible – even if he had been on time and not half an hour late. Perhaps if we'd stuck to my suggestion!

It was a terrific concert. A kind of music marathon against violence. Many of Poland's most popular rock bands were there including T-love, Sixteen, ONA, Budka Suflera, De Mono, all of which are on the *Spring 98* CD I bought from the markets on Saturday. In between the performances there were interviews and discussions projected onto a huge screen all about violence – violence on TV, in schools, between fans of opposing football teams etc. At the end everyone joined in singing a song about peace – quite uplifting.

It ended about 7 pm. I went home via Agnieszka's place to borrow some coconut for the ANZAC biscuits I was going to make for the class. I got straight into it when I got home but was so tired that I forgot to put the coconut in after all the trouble I'd gone to borrow it! But I sprinkled some on the top and nobody knew the difference. They loved it. I prepared a speech in Polish to explain the relevance of the biscuits – they were amused by my effort but applauded warmly.

I did, of course, call Mummy on Sunday night for her birthday and I got Agata and Edyta to sing *stolat* [happy birthday] with me. She loved it. They're online with their little palm-top now so what I was going to tell them has now become an email which I'll send tomorrow.

School today was quite interesting, not only because of the ANZAC biscuits. In the morning two busloads of Israeli students came to visit us. The visit was part of their eight-day tour of Poland which focuses on the historical sites of the Holocaust because many of them are descended from Polish Jews who escaped to Israel. It was very interesting to talk with them, in English of course. I exchanged email addresses with one particular girl, Yael, who also wants to be an architect. So now I have a friend in Israel.

The other interesting thing that happened was that a Polish writer came to talk to us about her work. I sat next to Martyna who transcribed what she said into English for me which was great because it was really interesting. She writes historical novels based on the experiences of Poles during the Holocaust. She talked about how lots of people contact her wanting their stories told, but she prefers to find her own characters, that she must not judge them or place herself above them, that she becomes really good friends with them, and a trust is established which eases the flow of communication. She doesn't tape the conversations but rather tries to absorb the feelings and atmosphere of what she's being told. Mostly her characters like the finished product but are often opposed to the way their character was described. I asked Martyna to ask her why she decided to dedicate her life to writing on this subject. She said that it's a kind of mission to inform people of the human side of it and not let them forget, so that history won't repeat itself. Very interesting.

28-4-98

Although I like Agata and Walenty very much, after being here three months I could do with a change of host family. Getting too comfortable can be dangerous I think. But it will be at least another three until I'll change I guess.

29-4-98

Life is sweet. Yes, I think I'm going to miss Terry and Jake when they leave. Tonight we went to the newly opened (today in fact) outdoor pub on Krakówskie Przedmieście. It's a really cool place and definitely a hot contender for an 18th birthday party venue. Before the meeting I went to the uni to send emails as I hadn't been able to do it at school today. I'm so glad now that I've been able to send all my emails. It's such a weight off my mind because it's been about two weeks since I sent any. So after that freeing experience I've been able to think about the near future with more optimism.

30-4-98

I had my first dream in Polish last night!

Walenty is starting to annoy me. He hardly talks to me or takes an interest in what I've been doing and when he does talk he likes to turn every conversation into an argument. For example, when I got home on Saturday night he said only two things to me. Firstly, that I had to go to Kraków tomorrow morning not tonight, as Agata was spending the night with friends half way to Kraków. (I had already decided to do so anyway). And when I asked if it would be possible to get a train to there, and go the rest of the way to Kraków with Agata, he thought I hadn't understood and went through it all again. I decided not to confuse the matter and just say that I would get the 7 am train and therefore get to Kraków about 10 am. Then he started to shout that that was too early. I tried to explain that there weren't any later ones. He shrugged. Then later, I had some compote which I had warmed on the stove. He ridiculed me for having it hot rather than cold. His facial expressions and gestures suggested he'd never heard of anything more stupid and he asked if we had hot compote in Australia. I said we don't have compote at all. He's a strange man. One of those that approaches things as if they're a problem. He even tries to find problems where none exist. No wonder Agata has started smoking again.

Kraków

From: jennifer phelan
Date: Fri, 8 May 1998
To: Judith
Subject: news from Poland

Dear Judith,

I've just got back from a spur of the moment trip to Kraków. I think the last
time I wrote I was going to be going camping with Martyna. Well that fell
through so I decided to take the opportunity to go by train to Kraków while
Agata was there on business. I arrived on Sunday morning just in time to
see the Constitution Day parade. Representatives of Poland's political parties
marched from the castle, through the main market square to a monument
on the other side. Half way they stopped to present flowers to the Cross of
Katyn – a monument to those who died in some conflict there – and there
was a bit of a kerfuffle when the Communist Party stepped forward to offer
theirs because they had been partly responsible for the deaths there.

In the afternoon Agata, her sister and I went for a walk in a nearby forest
where there was a small castle and some interesting rock formations.

On Monday I took myself off to Auschwitz (a 2 hour train trip). I'll write you
what I wrote in my diary about the experience. Visiting Auschwitz and
Birkenau was a somber experience. One that puts a frown on your forehead,
makes you bite your lip and fight back tears. I did the self-guided tour of
Auschwitz from the guide book I bought from the entrance, but on the

way picked up snippets from the tour guides who were leading groups of English speakers. I saw the 11 am screening of the 20 minute documentary in English – a poignant preparation for what we were about to see. I thought it somehow disrespectful that, as we were waiting for the film to begin, the American couple sitting behind me could only concern themselves with the hot chocolate that they were going to buy afterwards!

You can read all about the Holocaust in history books but nothing compares to walking where they walked, seeing where they slept, looking at the piles of possessions that were once theirs and finally, being inside the gas chamber where so many thousands perished. I encountered groups of German tourists and I thought to myself *It was your ancestors who were responsible for this.* I encountered American tourists and I thought to myself *It was your ancestors who refused to believe the reports of what was happening here.* Yet today this is irrelevant, it is the fact that it was human beings doing these terrible things to other human beings that is important. The very strong message that the camps portray is that it is up to us to prevent history repeating itself. As I was leaving Birkenau I spotted a young deer bounding playfully among the totemic chimney remains of the crematorium buildings. The ultimate image of life poignantly juxtaposed with that of death. I thought this highly significant in two ways. Firstly, as a reminder of life after death, that these victims found peace in heaven. Secondly as a reminder that we here now have life, the greatest gift of all!

Tuesday was miserable weather-wise and the museums are closed Mondays. But I bought some Dr Scholl's and had my hair cut. It's the shortest it's been since I was 4. I think I like it. At least it will be practical for travelling.

Wednesday morning I did 4 museums in 3 hours. The best was the Ethnographic museum in the old Jewish quarter of Kraków. I much prefer learning about how the average person lived rather than looking at displays of armour and furniture of royalty. There was a great collection of costumes from all the regions of Poland. Similarly house styles and egg painting patterns from the different regions. It's fascinating how regional Poland once was, and still is to some extent.

I got the train back to Warsaw in the afternoon and went straight to the Rotary meeting.

I'm very glad you're passing on my news to Doris and Mary. Mum and Dad are doing the same with the grandparents. This is very convenient as writing conventional letters is so unappealing to me now.

Until next time, *pa pa* (the colloquial goodbye)

Jennifer

Żoliborz

This is the second night in a row that I've stayed up past midnight typing emails. So then what do I do? Turn off the computer and write up my diary!

Anyway, Terry and Abby's farewell speech at the Rotary meeting last night was a big lesson for me in how not to do a farewell speech. Well, I mean, the two Americans presented it well, they'd prepared, and the skit they did was funny, entertaining and kind of cute, but there was just this undercurrent of ethnocentricity permeating the entire event. Talking about only differences and in a way that suggested anything that was not like it was in America was primitive. Of course, they probably didn't mean to do this, but some comments were highly tactless.

You know, there's another thing about my exchange that goes against the grain of common experience; I'm not growing apart from my friends back home, I think I'm actually becoming closer through our regular email contact.

It's quite ironic really that the young people my host parents have introduced me to, and have the utmost trust in, reveal their true selves away from adult presence. E.g. Pieter, Miranda and Mandek all smoke, drink and hide things from their parents. Meanwhile they put on this façade for the benefit of the adults. I think it's the fast pace of social change in Poland that has partly contributed to this wide generation gap. When something out of the ordinary does happen it comes as so much more of a shock.

Agata informed me that Mandek has moved out of home. This was the reason she stayed overnight with her friends on her way to Kraków as they needed to talk about it. He's twenty-something, has a job and will be getting married soon – which you would think are all characteristics of a person who should have moved out of home – but in Polish culture it's not like that. It's partly customary and partly due to the lack/cost of housing that young people live with their parents until marriage and often beyond, until their name comes up on the list for an apartment.

It's hard to believe that 10 years ago there was hardly anything in the shops. Now they're packed with almost everything and there are so many street stalls selling all sorts of things. Yet from the window of the train between Kraków and Warsaw you can see farmers ploughing their fields with horsepower and manpower. There's something romantic about doing it this way that can't be achieved with machinery.

I was like a zombie in school today and I think tomorrow is going to be the same at this rate – its 12.40 am!! What is it with me and writing? Why didn't I have this kind of flow for Related English last year!!??

10-5-98

It's such a nice feeling to get up in the morning and throw open the fat double-glazed windows and let in the beautiful spring morning. Then to sit on the wide windowsill in nighty and dressing gown and write in my diary... until I'm interrupted by the telephone – but it was Grandma – we had a nice chat.

I did my first test at school on Friday – maths, logarithms and I'm dreading the result because I didn't understand the parts written in Polish, so even though I solved the equations I don't know if that's what the questions were asking us to do.

You usually need a calculator for a maths test but I needed a dictionary. I just hope they don't brand all Australians as dumb when they see what mark I get.

12-5-98

One of the changes I've noticed in myself is that I've become much more of a people person than I ever was. I delight in the friends I have and the new ones I'm making. I was feeling a bit down this morning after two days moping around the house with a cold and it was the emails and phone calls from friends this afternoon that cheered me up.

On Sunday (before I got sick) Paweł and Jerzy (from my class at school) came at 4 pm and we rode our bikes along the Vistula to Wilanów on the other side of Warsaw. As we were at the furthest point from home I got a puncture and had to bus it home!

13-5-98

I wore my hemp dress today. The last time I wore it was at my leaving party in Australia – fond memories. I was thinking, too, that on Saturday when I wore my green skirt-and-top outfit that one of the last times I wore it was the day I went out to the Pizza Hut with my friends to celebrate our exam results. It's funny what memories clothes can trigger.

At the concert on Saturday, Jake mentioned that he's finding it even more difficult to make the effort to go to school now that the weather is so nice, and I agreed with him. But when I was thinking about it later I realised I wouldn't have been at the concert if I hadn't gone to school because it's there that I find out about these things. I suppose it's different for Jake with host siblings who also know what's going on in town.

14-5-98

It took me a while to realize that in Poland 'museum' is an art gallery and if you want what we understand as a museum you look for the words *'museum historyczne'*. Anyway, it wasn't worth going to school after seeing Terry and Abby off at the airport, so I went to Maria Sklodowska-Curie's museum in the Old Town. A simple display of photos, apparatus, awards, newspaper articles and postage stamps in her memory, but I felt I got to know her as a woman who was not only a ground-breaking scientist but also a sociologist, linguist, artist, writer, politician etc. I took down this visionary quote of hers which touched me for some reason:

'To develop science laboratories – which Pasteur called "holy shrines of humanity" – to facilitate the tasks of those who work for science, to extend care over the young who thirst for knowledge – and thus to gain workers of the future – to create conditions in which innate and precious talents may be realized and devoted to the service of ideals. This is the way to lead society along the path of developing its power, both spiritual and material.'

– Marie Sklodowska-Curie

I first learned about her when Mum bought me a book about her from a jumble sale when I was little. Today re-affirmed for me those feelings of aspiration and admiration I felt back then.

I want to make a note here that for my leaving speech I shouldn't talk about differences and similarities but rather whether goals have been achieved i.e. goals of the exchange program – take the word 'exchange' and express my hope that

I have given as much as I have received during the year, and my personal goals or reasons for coming on an exchange, which are:

* to be immersed in a culture different from my own and learn its language by being there as opposed to 'studying' it.

* to learn about myself, define who I am and what I want in life, and to see how I cope in a variety of different situations and challenges.

* to travel – to see and learn how the world works, how its people live, and how it came to be this way.

* to further Australia's international relations on a personal level by telling people about Australia.

Why am I thinking about this now? you ask, when I'm not yet four months into the exchange. Well, obviously it is an issue that has been brought to my mind by the recent bittersweet leaving speech of Terry and Abby, followed by their lacklustre departure.

17-5-98

It's true that as my Polish improves my English gets worse! It was rather embarrassing to be stuck for an English word and have it provided by a Polish lady. Yesterday I went to the International Book Fair at the Palace of Culture with Adela [a school friend]. It was very extensive, crowded with people and much more upmarket than I had expected. I bought James Michener's *Poland*, a CD for Mum, some postcards and some little hanging decoration thingies, plus I was in the right place at the right time to get a Polish garden diary/calendar. Adela is lovely and such an interesting person. Her uncle was born in Auschwitz and was the youngest person saved by Schindler! She told me about each Polish writer/poet as we came across their books. Unfortunately I couldn't find any Polish classics in English (plenty of English classics in Polish though!) There were books in French, German, Hebrew, Japanese etc, etc.

I made a realisation as to the reason I tend to answer in Polish when someone speaks to me in English, and answer in English when someone speaks to me in Polish. It's all to do with thinking time. If I've been busy translating what the person has said in Polish there would be a large break (which is usually taken to mean I didn't understand) while I translate my answer into Polish and say it. And vice versa, if someone has spoken in English I can be preparing a Polish answer while their last words are trailing off and answer straight away.

I got my maths test back on Friday: 4¼/24; oops. Oh well. It didn't even register for a point. It wasn't so much that it was very difficult but that I hadn't provided the 'conditions' for each question and, of course, hadn't studied.

When I got home after school, Pieter was here to see the letter and photos from Alojzy. He hadn't done as well as he'd hoped in his first two *Matura* exams. He has three more coming up in the next two weeks. He ate *obiad* with us then we both went to Marymont to buy a new inner tube for Alojzy's bike and he fixed it all up for me. While we were putting the new tyre on in the garage I happened to glance up and see my classmate Kasandra looking out of her kitchen window while she had a snack. I waved and called her over. Such a simple thing but being able to do this was a great feeling for me – have one friend there, call another over and introduce two Polish people who didn't know each other. I never had this neighbourly thing in Australia.

18-5-98

Exactly 4 months. A third of my exchange has passed! When I mentioned this to Agnieszka this afternoon she asked me 'So what do you like about Poland now that you've been here four months?' I thought, *I really ought to give some thought to this* and what better place to do it than in my diary. This should be done in a systematic way and it seems like everything will fit under the three headings of people, place and culture.

21-5-98

I didn't finish my last entry because Mum and Dad phoned. I'll finish my little task at a later date. It had been a while since we last talked – probably Easter – and I had been hoping they would call. Hearing their voices made me realise how much I miss them. It wasn't this so much that put me in a miserable, moping mood for the rest of the evening, but the sense I got through their voices that things are getting a bit heavy for them with the grandparents, and they're starting to snap at each other. But I am grateful that they don't live like Agata and Walenty – like two individual people in the one house with separate bedrooms and the only communication that occurs turns into an argument. They don't even tell each other where or when they are going/coming back or if someone phoned for them while they were out. It's a rather tense atmosphere to be living in, which is partly why I like to get out as much as possible. When they are relaxed and taken separately they are very nice. For instance on Sunday afternoon, Agata and I went on a little excursion south of Warsaw. We walked around the gardens of Wilanów (and had ice-cream there), walked around a recreation park not far from there (I had a go on a round-a-bout and afterwards tried to reassure Agata that, yes, I was turning 18 in three weeks!). The third stop was a place called Konstancin where we 'took the waters' of the natural spring. It was very interesting – a wooden construction with seats around its inside walls and two spraying machines in the middle distributing the water in a fine mist.

After school on Monday I went for a walk with Agnieszka and her dog. I don't usually like dogs but this one is small and timid. We were talking a mixture of Polish and English. Agnieszka would talk to the dog in Polish of course, but when she said 'Come' instead of '*Chodź tu*', we fell about laughing.

Agnieszka and I went around to all the outdoor pubs in the Old Town and on Krakówskie Przedmiescie asking about the cost of table reservations for 40 people on the 10th June. My personal first choice turned out to be the best option i.e., no cost for reservation and no quota on the amount that must be spent. I've been talking to a few people about the Polish customs in this situation and it seems like I will be expected to provide a round of beer for everyone – this will be rather expensive but perhaps it's the least I can do for all these people who have been so friendly and helpful to me.

The most exciting news is yesterday's happenings (Wednesday). I made my debut with Promni. We were being filmed for a special cultural program to be screened on Sunday 31st May. The setting was a mock-up of traditional cottages in Kampinos forest. I was dressed in traditional costume and was a 'background dancer' for three or four scenes. It was great fun but rather tiring because of all the takes we had to do in the heavy costumes and warm weather. For lunch we walked through the forest a little way to a little shack and were served a bowl of Polish soup which we ate in the company of Polish mosquitos, to the sound of Polish birds, in a Polish forest, dressed in Polish costume... It was all very... Polish!

When I got home Agata and Walenty were out. There were two phone calls before they got back. One was a man who I took a message from and thought I had understood correctly. I took down the number that he said and the time to call. When Agata read the message she was very puzzled, looked at me and said 'But this is our number.' I looked and so it was. I laughed at what I had stupidly done. Agata said, 'So do you want me to go into the city and call here?'

23-5-98

The thoughts and images in my mind are running on like a TV show that won't let me go back and review something I missed! It's 1.10 am, I should really have written 24-5-98. I've just got back from Madlen's 18th party. Half the class was there and it was quite fun. Kasandra also had her 18th party tonight so the class was split according to allegiance. I decided to go to the same one as Agnieszka chose. I taught them the 'Nutbush' and the 'Bus Stop'.

25-5-98

School is definitely a challenge of endurance these days. With the end of the academic year approaching there is exam tension in the air which is certainly not a pleasant environment to be in.

Yesterday was a bit of an endurance effort too. I went with Promni to a country town two hours bus trip away where they were to perform for the anniversary of a fire station. We waited for ages until it was their turn to go on, but they provided us with beer and *obiad*. The weather was awful – cold and rainy. I attempted to go for a little walk while we were waiting but soon turned back when the rain got heavier. They did a good job in the tiny space provided for them and the crowd was in stitches when one of the girls lost her underskirt! The atmosphere on the bus coming home was very merry in both senses of the word. The burly chap (don't remember his name) was doing the rounds with the vodka bottle and there was no refusing him! I chatted away with Paweł who's a little egotistical but cute and very nice. Then they started singing Polish songs which was quite entertaining. I felt a bit like a tag-along and wanted to be useful so helped to carry the suitcases to the bus after the performance. This caused quite a stir – a girl carrying the cases. It was an outrage. 'That's the boys' job,' they told me. 'Leave them, you're a girl.' And several boys tried to take them from me. My refusal meant I was instantly branded a feminist. My shock and surprise caused me to kick one guy in the shins before I realised what I did. Should I conform to what is obviously quite a strong Polish custom or stick up for women? It's a tough one.

29-5-98

I took the day off school on Wednesday and went with Miranda to the solarium. I probably won't go again but I had to go once for the experience since it's such a cultural institution in Poland. (And I got a burnt bum!)

Agata and Miranda left soon after midday for Kraków. Agata said she would return on Friday evening. I raised my eyebrows sceptically saying 'I'll believe it when I see it', because whenever she goes to Kraków she never returns the day she says she will. 'No, I have to come back Friday' she assured me, 'I have an important appointment on Saturday.' But I was right – she hadn't returned by the time I left for Prague!

On Monday I had sent an email to Ron requesting a favour concerning Alojzy's visa on behalf of Agata and Walenty. On

Wednesday I received a reply. In a sudden and surprising show of his joy and appreciation Walenty threw his arms around me and gave me a big hug when I told him in Polish that Ron had called Alojzy and that everything would be OK. An 18-year-old guy who's been in Australia for nine months can't sort himself out but I, from the other side of the world, can pull a few strings and have everything sorted in a matter of days. That sounds so super-womanish and like I'm big-noting myself when I read back over that last sentence. I just find it rather incredulous that they can make such a big deal out of a problem whose solution is so easy. In fact I think that's a characteristic of Polish people in general – they do like making a fuss out of nothing.

Prague

From: jennifer phelan
Date: Wed, 03 June 1998
To: group email
Subject: Prague

I'm back from Prague and it was great! My only regret is that we didn't spend longer there.

The group consisted of my class plus the boyfriends of some of the girls and a handful of girls from one of the other classes. There were 2 teachers, 2 bus drivers and a tour guide. We left at 7 am on Saturday morning and after 11 hours in the coach arrived in the Czech mountains just the other side of the border where we were to spend the first night. The chateau we stayed in was surrounded by a forest of towering fir trees. After dinner we had a little stroll outside between rain showers.

We left really early on Sunday morning and our first stop was Moravsky Kras where we took a tour of the caves with their impressive stalactites and stalagmites. Part of it was a boat ride along an underground river. In the early afternoon we were in Slavkov u Brna (Austerlitz) – Napoleon Bonaparte country. Here we had a tour of the baroque palace where Napoleon spent 4 days concluding the armistice of 'the battle of the Three Emperors'. We arrived in Prague in the evening and stayed at a cheap hotel out of the centre.

Monday and Tuesday were two full days spent in Prague itself. Our tour guide took us around the old town square and the Jewish quarter in the morning. I stayed close to her and after she talked to the group in Polish she told me in English. In the afternoon we had free time. I went with two girls to the Karluv Bridge – Prague's oldest bridge linking the two sides of the city which are divided by the Vltava River. It had witnessed many battles and is now a footbridge alive with tourists and artists selling their wares. The view from its tower is fantastic – all the red rooves, narrow winding lanes, majestic towers and green hills in the background.

In the evening we met up again and went to Prague's oldest beer gardens (since 1491) to sample Czech beer. After dinner we went to a water and musical spectacular. A fountain with coloured lights 'danced' to music. It was pretty but a little monotonous.

On Tuesday our guide took us along the 'Royal Way' from the gate to old town, through the old market square, over the bridge and up the hill to the castle. It is the largest castle in central Europe and was certainly very impressive. Again the view was breathtaking. The majestic gothic church near the entrance is fantastic, and then there's what they call the Golden Lane on the other side. A lane of tiny cottages all squashed together where the tradesmen used to live.

During the free time in the afternoon I took the Metro to an area south of Prague called Vysehrad – a citadel from where you can admire Prague from a distance. We met up again in the evening for a stroll around Prague at night – beautiful!

At 10.30 pm we left romantic Prague behind and travelled by night back to Warsaw.

It was a little difficult having to conform to the group itinerary after being used to planning everything myself, but it was a great experience. Unfortunately we didn't see any museums or classical music concerts but it gave me a taste of Prague – a city I'll probably go back to one day.

Bye for now.

Jennifer

Żoliborz

6-6-98

Life is one big PARTY!

So, the Rotary picnic. It was great fun. Gorgeous weather – so hot (35°C) I even got sunburnt. This event is Warsaw Rotary Club's major annual fundraising event and reminded me a bit of 'Jazz in the Vines' in the Hunter Valley in that it took place on a property in the country and involved a lot of people, music and food (and free beer for the workers!) I arrived at 10 am and was helping sell raffle/parking tickets for a few hours. After that I just had a good time with the other young people there. It was like a big reunion of exchange students. Past Rotary exchange students were there including Alina and Tym. Rotaract members were also there (there are two small groups in Warsaw). I met a girl from Cabramatta! She was born in Poland but has lived in Australia since she was not yet one. She's staying with family in Warsaw for four months between college and work. Small world ain't it? It was great to hear an Aussie accent again.

I met Marysia, the next Polish exchange student to Australia following Alojzy. She had a lot of questions and seems rather timid and afraid of the concept. We're meeting this Friday. I'll show her photos, Alojzy's video and answer any questions she has. They really don't prepare their students here – she hadn't even met Alina. It was me who introduced them. Also at the picnic were two girls from USA who were exchange students here two years ago and are back for a visit. The 3 exchange students from Brazil got together with returned Polish exchange students to Brazil and while we were waiting for the fireworks to begin started singing Brazilian songs. Alina, Sylvia (the girl from Sydney) and I tried to drown them out with 'I Feel Like a Toohey's' and 'Waltzing Matilda'. It was so funny. Kasandra from over the back was also there with her friends and during the day I bumped into Mina from school, so altogether it was a rather social day.

11-6-98

Talk about an adrenaline rush! Whoah!! My 18th went off with a bang. It was a day of continuous celebration climaxing with the party in *14 klub* in the evening. It was an incredible experience to see all the friends I've made over the last five months all at once. And the presents! I was totally overwhelmed. But I should start from the beginning. I woke up about 7 am and it took me a couple of minutes before I remembered it was my birthday. I got up, showered, dressed and ate breakfast. Mum and Dad called, followed by a call from Auntie Judith. I went to prepare the chocolates I had bought to take to school, only to find that half of them had melted, so I went to school via Globi supermarket to get some more. The first lesson was History with our homeroom teacher. When there was a lull I approached her and announced my birthday – everybody stood and sang:

sto lat, sto lat	100 years, 100 years
niech żyje żyje nam	May they live
sto lat, sto lat	100 years, 100 years
niech żyje żyje nam	May they live
jeszcze raz, jeszcze raz	Once again, once again
niech żyje żyje nam	May they live
niech żyje nam	May they live

It was terrific. Then, as the tradition goes, I went around to each individual. They wished me all the best, we kissed three times on the cheek then they took a sweet from my box. I worked out that I must have received about 400 kisses in total during the day because it is the custom to greet guests in such a way when they arrive and leave the party. I rather like this custom.

The last lesson was cancelled for half of the class who had English, so I went home to help Agata with the preparations for *obiad* which was scheduled for 2 pm. We took everything out into the back garden and soon after Pieter and Jake arrived. The phone kept ringing all afternoon.

So at the party there were my closest friends, but I must admit it was very difficult for me to choose as my limit was seven including me: Agnieszka, Marcel, Madlen, Martyna, Pieter and Jake. They blended really well. We sat around the table in the garden and ate grilled *kiełbasa* [sausage] with mustard, bread and salad. It suddenly began to rain when we were halfway through our meal. Pieter raced into the garage and got the umbrella but it came heavier so we got a sheet of plastic and threw it over to make like a tent. So there we were, seven people squashed under a plastic canopy in the middle of a large garden eating *obiad* while the rain fell around us! Quite a strange but memorable situation. Thankfully it didn't last long and when we'd finished eating we went upstairs for champagne and birthday cake. Of course we were talking all the time in Polish and it was quite funny earlier when there were phone calls from Australia and England, having to divert back to English. In fact, when I was talking to Nana, I was half listening to the conversation going on around me and then I started to talk to Nana in Polish.

The cake was absolutely beautiful – rich and richly decorated with '18 *lat*' on a sugar wafer. Complemented very nicely with Russian Champagne. After this we watched the video of me on

TV with Promni. I forgot to mention the balloons – Mum and Dad sent me a packet of eight balloons (four blue, four green) each with '18 today' printed on them. I tied two to the gate, two at the side of the house, two to the tree and two to the table.

By this time it was about 5 pm so Agnieszka, Marcel, Madlen and Martyna went home leaving Pieter and Jake, who entertained themselves while I got myself looking lovely for the evening. When I was ready the three of us left together (me carrying the carrot cake), unfortunately leaving behind a rather large mess for Agata to clear up.

At Rotary my speech and the carrot cake were a great success. I forgot to ask someone to take a photo. In fact I regret not taking more photos of the whole day but I have my memories and this detailed account – how could I ever forget it anyway?

When we arrived at the pub we were confronted with a problem. The guy I had made the reservation with was not present, and the guys who were there knew nothing about any reservation. Consequently most of the tables outside (where I wanted to be) were already occupied. They said we could have the whole downstairs with the keg and chips for 400 zł. I accepted as I really didn't have any alternative. It was very hot but had cool décor and music. As I said I was absolutely overwhelmed with the number of presents I got – they just kept coming. And they weren't just spur-of-the-moment gifts – a lot of thought and creativity had been put into it. They were even lining up to give me their presents, and by the end a whole corner of the club was filled with flowers, books, jewellery, a balloon, ornaments, writing paper, a cushion... Tymon gave me 'something to help with my Polish' – a bottle of Polish vodka! But the best gift of all was the '18' sign from the number 18 tram which Mandek had stolen the previous night and signed. Afterwards others signed it too. It has no use and is rather cumbersome but strangely enough it was what I had been hoping for most because it's a Polish tradition, and of course highly appreciated due to the difficulty in obtaining it. Mandek rode the line twice in the dark before he could snatch it with the minimum of witnesses. Something I will treasure forever.

Obviously, there was no way I was going to be able to take all these things home on a bus. Paweł came to the rescue – he had his car. It meant I had to leave at about 11 pm but most people had left by then anyway. I'm glad it didn't drag on actually because it was a quality few hours, and also meant I got a few hours' sleep before heading off to Mazury today. I managed to mingle and share myself around with everyone. Unavoidably groups formed but it was a pleasure for me to see people enjoying themselves. So everyone had one free beer on me then it was up to them if they wanted more. Mandek bought me a shot of vodka and one for himself and introduced me to another Polish tradition. He said that to make the transition from acquaintance to friend you must drink a shot of vodka together like thus: link arms, scull the vodka, say your own name and then kiss each other on the cheek. After this you can call each other by first names.

There was a bit of dancing. Mandek danced with me. He said Paweł wanted to but was too shy. In fact I had seen Mandek trying to persuade him to ask me earlier but gave up and danced with me himself instead. I have to say that Annette is one very lucky girl to have Mandek.

You know, I think I've grown away from Jake quite significantly. I don't like myself in his company and his humour is lacking. I'm now seeing a very critical person, a slight pessimism and disinterest. Was I blind before when I saw in him the qualities of a good sense of humour, someone who didn't judge and highly optimistic? I think I'm falling in love with Tym. He's so full of compliments. Not as funny as Mandek but certainly more than Jake. And so helpful. In fact I am indebted to him and Pieter for sorting out the problem with the reservation.

Mandek, Paweł and Jerzy were so good to me. They took all my presents to the car, drove me home, then helped me take them all upstairs. As it was only 11.30 pm, and I said I'd be home at 2 am, Agata and Walenty were still up. Agata put all my bouquets in vases (using all the vases she possessed) and we made a display of all the presents and flowers on the table for me to take a picture of. I still can't get over it. I went to admire them all again this morning, before I left.

'Was it a vision or a waking dream?
Fled is that music
Do I wake or sleep?'
[John Keats, 'Ode to A Nightingale']

I didn't get to bed until 1.30 am as I had to pack my gear for camping for the school kayak trip. I woke up at 4.30 pm with a start as I was so worried I'd sleep in and miss the trip. I nearly missed it anyway because neither Agata nor Walenty knew where the West Station was.

I should write about Friday – the last day of school and quite a busy one for me. I went to school at 9 am for the final day ceremony dressed (as you do) in black or blue and white. Although everyone was dressed smartly it was a rather casual affair. Firstly everyone assembled in the *basen* [pool area] and the *Dyrektor* gave a speech analysing how the class had performed this year, presenting books to the best student in each class, and finishing by wishing everyone a great summer holiday. After this there was a bit of a skit put on by first-year students, and then we went to our classes where our teacher presented each student with their *świadectwo* [Graduation Certificate]. The students then presented the teacher with flowers. The whole thing was finished by 10.45 am so I went home and began to prepare, as I had invited Marysia for *obiad*. I went to meet her at 1 pm and we spent the afternoon talking about Australia, Rotary exchange, looking at photos and watching part of Alojzy's video. She had plenty of questions for me and I think she really appreciated my help. She reminds me of me before I left Australia – strong and independent on the inside but a little timid and afraid on the outside. I think she'll be a great exchange student, she's a lovely girl and I'll meet her in Australia when I go back in January.

Mazurian Lakes

From: jennifer phelan
Date: Tue, 16 June 1998
To: Judith
Subject: Thanks heaps!

I've just returned from 5 days camping and kayaking in the Mazurian Lake
district of N.E. Poland. Such is the reason for my delay in thanking you for
your kind birthday wishes and present. The camera is still performing very
well. I've averaged about a film every 3 weeks so there'll be plenty to show
when I return!

After my birthday party I had 3 hours sleep and then was up and off to
Mazury with a group from school. It was a 5 hour train trip followed by
2 hours on a bus to the point where we would begin our journey. It was
quite a challenging expedition kayaking all day along rivers and lakes and
camping each night. Everything had to be carried with us in the kayaks
securely wrapped in plastic bags. Even when camping the male and female
roles are distinct. The girls will not pull the kayaks onto land or carry logs for
the fire but they will prepare sandwiches for the boys. It rained every day
but that didn't spoil too much the beauty and tranquillity of the place, and
altogether it was a rewarding experience.

I went swimming for the first time in 5 months a couple of weeks ago. I took
the day off school (again) and went with Mia (my German friend from Polish
lessons) and her cousin to a lake about 20 minutes from Warsaw. It was a
really nice relaxing day just swimming, sunbathing and eating our picnic.

Plenty of mozzies though! I thought they didn't have them in Poland but I was wrong and they seem to like foreign blood! – an exotic meal!!!

As you know, on Saturday I'm off to England for a week, culminating with an 18th party with friends and family there. It will be my third 18th party – each one having been held in a different country! My friends in Australia had one in my absence and sent me the video!!

Thanks again.

Na razy (see ya)
The 18 year old.

Jennifer

Żoliborz

I do feel different being 18. I feel like an adult now. Over these past five months (and it's exactly five months today) I think I have matured a fair bit, become more certain of who I am and become even more independent. I basically don't rely on anybody anymore. I do my own washing, ironing, cleaning, cooking, food shopping, plan my own trips, outings…

When I returned from the kayaking trip, Agata had already gone to Kraków. She'd left me a note and 50 zł saying 'buy what food and drink you need.' The problem was she hadn't told Walenty about this. After school on Wednesday, like a responsible exchange student, I go grocery shopping then start to prepare *obiad*. Then Walenty comes home with groceries (almost exactly the same things as I have bought) criticises me for it, then starts criticising the way I'm cutting the potatoes and whatever else he can find to criticise. I got really pissed off. Then he asks me when Agata will be back. I felt like saying, *you're her husband, I'm the exchange student staying in your house who has just got back from a camping trip and you ask me when Agata's going to be back from Kraków?* Anyway, it didn't bother me for too long – I got over it pretty quickly. There's too many other exciting things happening for me to waste time and energy holding grudges.

I wrote my contribution for *Travellers' Tales* [the newsletter for Australian Rotary Youth Exchange students], then headed off across town to meet Mariusz, Fiona's friend who has invited me to join a children's Summer English camp in the Tatra Mountains during the first half of August as a teacher/counsellor. He told me about the program for the camp, the staff, and what my responsibilities would be. He asked me some general questions and I asked my questions also. He gave me all the info I needed, asked me to do a bit of research, then we exchanged phone numbers and emails and parted with the mutual agreement that we had a deal. Then it was off to Rotary for me.

The Brazilians and Jake don't have much time left. 18 days in fact for Jake. He doesn't want to leave. We were talking about it over a beer at the outdoor pub this afternoon between emailing and Polish lesson. He said he's going to miss Europe as a whole – the closeness of things. The sense that I have of feeling more mature is rather timely as I'm soon to become the 'leader' as the next batch of exchange students from Brazil and America come to Poland in August.

This evening was my last Polish lesson. Our teacher made a pretend toast to me and asked me what I wanted to wish for. I wished that the 2nd half of my exchange would be as good as the first. I was thinking about this in terms of recognising how lucky I am, wondering what I have done to deserve all this generosity and kindness endowed upon me. That everything in my life goes right – fits into place. And then I thought of Shakespeare's words:

'There's nothing either good or bad but thinking makes it so.'
[Shakespeare, *Hamlet*]

I wonder if someone else who had my life, but not my way of thinking, would enjoy it as much as I am.

England

I was so nervous about meeting Mum and Dad again. I've no idea why. I didn't know what I would say, how I would (should?) behave. But I had no need to worry, we gelled immediately and it was like the old three-some again. The plane touched down at exactly 17.45 but I had to wait half an hour for my bag. Mum gave a little jump for joy when I walked through the door and I felt my face transform into a beaming smile that couldn't be wiped off.

We stayed the night at a delightful B&B about one hour north of London. A kind and obliging man and his wife made us feel very welcome in their beautifully adapted old cottage. They fed us a full English breakfast the next morning, giving us a great start to the day. Firstly we went for a long walk nearby which crossed through Chequers (the Prime Minister's weekend country residence). Then we drove to Wrest Park – a lovely manor house with formal gardens. Here we had some of the Czech beer and *pączek* I brought. We strolled around the grounds, at one stage joining the audience for a moving theatrical performance of *Alice in Wonderland*. (That's moving in terms of not stationary rather than poignant.)

The drive to Grandma and Grandpa's then took 2½ hours. It has been a beautiful sunny day too. This evening we watched the video of me on TV (the culture program we did with Promni). I was a bit disappointed in the reactions. They weren't all that enthusiastic about it, but I suppose that was partly because they didn't understand what was being said.

Even though Mum and Dad said they didn't want to talk about grandparents, over these past two days they inevitably came up in the conversation, and they ended up telling me about the difficulties they've been having with them. I've seen some evidence already tonight of the fuddy-duddiness and fussing that are their characteristics.

We had a very interesting conversation about homesickness in the car as Mum and Dad said they feel very homesick for Australia. I came to the conclusion that there are three categories of homesickness: people, place and culture. When you're away from the people, place and culture that you know, homesickness sets in when you don't involve yourself in the new people, places and culture. I think it is by doing this that I have never felt homesick. Mum and Dad said it was the best decision they ever made, moving to Australia – and I agree.

25-6-98

Feeling a bit sick and sorry for myself. Today's intended trip to Glasgow with Mum, Dad, Nana and Grandad had to be cancelled as I have a dose of the flu. But it's given me a chance to write about the activities of the past few days before I get even further behind.

On Monday we had a day trip around Yorkshire with Grandma and Grandpa. We visited Theakston's brewery in Ripon. Quite small and low key compared with Guinness in Dublin but very interesting. The furthest point of our journey was the Wensleydale cheese factory. We were unfortunately too late for a factory tour but we bought some cheese and looked at all the *Wallace and Gromit* souvenirs. I bought a W&G pin for my blazer. We had a little picnic with our cheese and hot cross buns by a bubbling brook in the countryside.

That evening Mummy and Daddy presented me with their main present for my birthday. A Psion computer much like theirs. So, if I find a server in Poland I'll be able to email from home!

On Tuesday Mum, Dad and I spent most of the day in Goathland, otherwise known as Aidensfield from the *Heartbeat* TV series. We had a drink in the Aidensfield Arms and ate a stottie over the road. We watched the steam train come in, looked around the visitor centre and the village in general. Then we had a walk to the remains of the Roman Road nearby.

We arrived at Nana and Grandad's place in Seaham at about 7 pm. It was so nice to have someone really interested in seeing my photos and asking intelligent questions. With Grandma it was either complaining that I was too quiet or making prejudiced assumptions about Poland, which it was my job to contradict.

We spent yesterday in Sunderland only seven miles from Seaham where there was much interest in a concentrated area. We began at the Glass Centre, a new building on the harbour which comprises of glass museum (not yet completed) and glass gallery, restaurant, glass blowing demonstrations and gift shop. The displays are fantastic and the building is terrific, modern and airy. We took a walk along the foreshore which has recently been done up and incorporates a series of sculptures with a maritime flavour. After this we looked in at the nearby St. Peters church dating from the 600s where the first glass in Britain was made. There is a fascinating history attached to the building which is very informatively displayed in their visitors' centre. In the evening, after tea, we went for a walk along the beach and collected glass pebbles which I am going to put in a bottle with oil.

26-6-98

I wanna go home! Back to Poland that is. I feel much more Polish than I do English which is rather ironic since I'm full-blooded English. Australian is what I am but for this year Poland is 'home'. I guess the miserable weather has a lot to do with my dissatisfaction. It's unfortunate that we haven't been able to go to Glasgow and Lindisfarne while we've been here but that can't be helped.

30-6-98

I'm leaving behind the oldness and slowness of England where conversations are insubstantial and illness abounds, and returning to youthful, vibrant Warsaw where I feel healthy and at home. Mum and Dad said they would try their best to make it a pleasurable trip and not just a duty visit, but it was inevitable that it was going to feel like a duty visit anyway. As I said when I was saying goodbye to Mum – I've felt with Mum and Dad that I've been visiting friends rather than parents which has been lovely, but this is not the same with grandparents. Sure I love them as family but not as friends which is hardly surprising when we've lived half a world away for most of my life. The party that Mum and Dad arranged for me was great. Funnily enough I received an abundance of bracelets – the chains of duty?

'I made a garland for her head
 And bracelets too, and fragrant zone.'
 [John Keats, 'La Belle Dame sans Merci']

I don't feel duty-bound by the lovely people who travelled (many of them) three or four hours to be at the White Horse pub in Yorkshire for the celebration, nor begrudge them. No. It was really nice to have 'the English contingent' all together in the one place at the one time. I felt very honoured but at the same time a little nervous and unsure, seeing again my godparents and my babysitter from long ago, who represent my Englishness as well as the childhood I'm leaving behind. Mixed in with all those feelings was the feeling of wonderment at what I had done to deserve such attention. Sometimes when I'm writing my diary I think of *Zlata's Diary* written by the young Bosnian girl Zlata Filipovic and think what a contrast mine is in comparison. Full of tales of adventure, excitement and happiness, travel and discovery, where hers was filled with tales of fear, horror and grief, confinement and loss in a war-stricken country. My grandparents didn't forget to remind me of the hardships they suffered in war times during adolescence – Grandma almost begrudgingly but Nana's attitude was 'Make the most of your freedom.' 'I'm doing that' I assured her.

Żoliborz

30-6-98 (continued)

So much for all that. I get back to Warsaw and it's deserted. Everyone's gone – skeleton staff only.

Philippa has sent me a tape of Aussie songs – fabulous timing. I was needing some resources for the English camp in August.

'Carra Barra Wirra Canna
Little star upon the lake
Guide me through the hours of darkness
Keep me safe until I wake.'
[Rolf Harris, 'Carra Barra Wirra Canna']

1-7-98

The trip to the Lakes has fallen through. The reason is that a huge farewell party is being organised for Jake and the Brazilian girls on Sunday at the property of one of the rich Rotarian guys and we are obliged to attend. Not that I'd knock back an *impreza*! Tym's going to give me a lift – two hours in the car with Tym, I can't wait. I spent this evening with him – he is sooo nice. We met at Rotary then I went back to his place to use his computer for emailing purposes. I made an assumption that the uni computer room would be closed for the vacation – an assumption that has turned out to be wrong, but if I had checked I wouldn't have gone to Tym's this evening. The emailing didn't take long. We chatted about experiences, Australia, cultural differences, and other exchange students. He is such a charmer. I missed the last bus home and he had to drive me home – what a shame! But nothing has happened... yet!!

2-7-98

How is it that my host sister, who is full-blooded Polish, can avoid a fine for not having a bus ticket by putting on the foreigner act, yet I, who have no Polish blood whatsoever, cannot convince the ticket inspectors that I'm not Polish, no matter how much English I speak?

Alojzy comes home on Monday – yeh! Jake leaves on Monday – hmmm!

I can't stop thinking about Tym! Smitten, I think, is the word!

5-7-98

TRUDNO. KURCZA. BOZE. JEZU.

Bad words. I've just got back from the party that was organised as a kind of farewell for the Brazilian girls and Jake (yet Jake wasn't there). These Americans are good at being absent from their own farewell parties. Anyway, I came so close to kissing Tym...but it didn't happen. The party itself was pretty boring. The Brazilians, who had brought a few friends, kept to themselves and then there was Tym, Alina, and me. Oh, and my host sister-to-be was there for a while too. The adults left us alone in this kind of hut thing on the property, which had no walls but a fire in the corner. It rained on and off all day and was rather cold. They fed us soggy food and gross French wine but when the adults left we found some beer and turned the stereo up. We danced a bit but most of the time we were sitting around talking and eating. By 7 pm we'd had enough. Tym drove Alina, and I home. He dropped me off last and it was then that I came so close. Even though we'd been dropping hints all day (what I took as hints anyway) I wasn't absolutely sure he liked me because it could just be his way, but when we arrived at my place we'd been talking about our plans for the vacation and I said I probably wouldn't see him for a while. He said 'You're breaking my heart'. He put his hand on my knee but I kissed him on the cheek as normal, not the lips, and got out of the car.

The thing is, I like to be the one doing the chasing, the one in control. I didn't feel like I was in control. But where does that get me? Nowhere. Here in my bedroom pouring it all out into a letter to Philippa and repeating it here in my diary. As I said to Philippa, I'm in love but have nobody to talk about it with. I have to put it behind me now – my stupid mind jumps to the vain hope that he'll go against what he said and be at the airport in the morning to see Jake off. But what would I do if he was? Owwwwww! I wish I could turn the clock back!!

7-7-98

Well, the day that for some time had hung in the distance, wrapped in dread and joy simultaneously, has finally passed. The departure of Jake and the arrival of Alojzy. After only two hours of sleep (Lord only knows why) I was up and off to the airport arriving about 7 am. It was a quiet affair. The emptiness and melancholia I felt were not simply caused by Jake leaving but the realisation that my year is almost half over. Zombie-like I headed back into the city which was shrouded in a thick, grey, ugly smog. Buses smashed through puddles, spraying unsuspecting pedestrians on the sidewalk, and rain fell.

It was then time to snap out of it and help with the preparations for Alojzy's homecoming. As my anger decreased with each chop of the vegetables, my happiness edged its way up. Walenty looked 10 years younger as he watched the preparations taking place around him, and Agata, although she was nervously flitting here and there, had a huge smile on her face and was in extremely good humour. As we left the house at 3 pm, it was like a new day. The sun was shining and all thoughts of the morning had been forgotten. I was ready with the camera as a smiling, tanned, long-haired Alojzy came through the doors. There were 10 of us for *obiad* and the food just kept coming and coming. I think Agata was on a mission to give Alojzy every traditional Polish dish in the first meal. I was very quiet, just listening, observing (and trying to stay awake). The adrenaline kept me going but when I got into bed I was asleep as soon as my head hit the pillow.

8-7-98

Italy here I come! All packed and ready to go. In a few minutes Agata will drive me to the station.

It was great to see Alojzy again but I think the reason I kind of went back into myself was because he was a part of my past and the old me was being recreated. One of the things Tym and I were discussing is the fact that when you go on exchange you have no 'past' in your new country and you can decide to be what you like.

Italy

From: jennifer phelan
Date: Thu, 30 Jul 1998
To: group email
Subject: ROMEING IN ITALY

For two and a half weeks I did what many Polish people do during the summer vacation – I went to Italy. I backpacked around with fellow Aussie exchange student – Kylie. Unlike my last trip, this time we concentrated on one country but what a varied time we had!

It was quite an education in the history of architecture. From the Roman ruins of Pompeii, 'frozen' in time by the eruption of Mt. Vesuvius in 79 AD to the colourful, Moorish-looking houses of Sorrento and Capri. From the world's largest gothic cathedral in Milan to the grandiose baroque St. Peter's cathedral in the Vatican. From the narrow streets and canals lined with flower-decked balconies in Venice to the large sculptural Renaissance buildings of Florence. And of course the precarious Leaning Tower of Pisa. All this only increased my desire to study architecture.

Art galleries, naturally, featured heavily in the itinerary. We saw Leonardo's *Last Supper* in Milan, Michelangelo's *Creation* on the ceiling of the Sistine Chapel and his *David* sculpture in Florence. It was quite a buzz to see many of the works I had studied in Art at high school.

It could be said that our trip was a bit of a religious pilgrimage also. We visited a great deal of churches but they were more a tourist attraction than a place of worship. Many of them afforded fantastic views from the top. We walked on the roof of Milan's gothic cathedral, and had a great view of Florence from its gothic cathedral.

A literary pilgrimage was another aspect of the trip. We saw Desdemona's house in Venice (from my Year 11 Shakespeare text: *Othello*), in Verona we visited Juliet's balcony (Year 10 Shakespeare text *Romeo and Juliet*) and in Rome we paid our respects to Keats (Year 12 poet), visiting his grave in Rome's Protestant Cemetery and museum situated in the house in which he died.

And of course it was a gastronomic tour. We found the best pizza in Sorrento and I even had a go at making one with the chef. We can probably say we're experts in gelati now too! A-gelato-a-day was pre-programmed into our budget.

Although we planned our trip pretty well we still had room for spontaneity. On our last afternoon in Rome we came across rollerblades for hire in the park, so for an hour we explored the park on wheels. It was Kylie's first time. She was doing so well until 10 minutes before the end when she fell and grazed her leg. So I got to play nurse and use my first aid kit. On one of our afternoons in Venice, we took a boat out to one of the outer islands which we explored on bikes.

Our experience of the Mediterranean beaches in the south made us realise how lucky we are in Australia. It took us a while to find a spare patch of pebbles and it was not much fun swimming almost shoulder to shoulder with everyone else in murky water. Yet it is such an institution in Italy. There are very few free beaches. Most people pay to have their own little beach hut which line the beaches in neat rows. But it was an experience and we can say we've swum in the Mediterranean!

We met many fellow backpackers in the campsites and hostels we stayed at, including a busload of Aussies! Everywhere we went I met Polish people, we even joined a Polish tour group for a few minutes going around the Pompeii ruins and I translated for Kylie!

I think I've returned from this trip feeling more sure of myself and proud to be Australian. It was the first real contact I'd had with an Aussie in six months and it was great to talk 'strayn' again! We celebrated the date of six months since leaving Australia with a special meal in Sorrento. I'm refreshed, renewed and determined not to waste a minute of the next six months.

Żoliborz

Back to deathly silent, dull, grey Warsaw where to speak on the bus seems sinful. Just when I felt I needed a bit of love after two nights on the train I arrive to find nobody at home. In the six hours I had in Budapest at Kylie's place, between trains, I was unable to get through to tell them I'd be home today and hence no one is home.

I go from one day feeling utterly alone in the world to the next feeling a little over-loved. There seems to be a competition on to be my next host family. I spent most of today with Marysia at her house in Podkowa Leśna right near where my next host family live. Apparently they had been told they would be hosting me and are now very upset that they're not. I was endowed with food and kisses and smiles and presents by Marysia's mother and promises of trips here and there with them. Plus they've already invited me to spend Christmas with them. She's really appreciative of the help I've given Marysia, who will leave for Australia in less than a month (22 August). They have a gorgeous house – old and rather stately, but they have only owned it since April and are currently renovating. It's in a lovely spot too surrounded by forest. I got a translation of the town's name today from Marysia. She told me it means horseshoe forest.

That's exactly what it is – a town surrounded by this horse-shoe-shaped forest. It will be so different from living in Warsaw. All this change is so exciting.

When I called Tym last night (who is away) and talked to his sister, she told me that they want to host me later in the year too. This is all news to me.

29-7-98

Another family has joined the competition to host me – the new counsellor for exchange students whose son is going to America. I met him last night.

Today rushing here and there emailing, packing etc, I felt like I was going to burst, but a phone call two minutes ago dashed my hopes of getting out of this house. My new host sister had a problem with her teeth so I can't go tonight.

I really can't stand Walenty anymore. What hurt me more than anything he's ever done before was this morning when he made a farcical imitation of my friend. I can handle him making criticisms of me but when he starts criticising my friends that's just too much. He really doesn't think. He asked me again today the very familiar question 'When will Agata be back?' As always I said I didn't know, but this time I decided to question why he didn't know. His answer was that she didn't know herself because she was supervising some repair work in the Kraków apartment and doesn't know how long it will take. So if she doesn't know herself how the hell am I supposed to know for God's sake?

30-7-98

I can't believe Walenty. When I told him last night that I wasn't leaving because my sister has a problem with her teeth he didn't believe me saying 'No, there must be some other problem, that's just an excuse.' As if to say it's really that they don't want me. Then he demanded their telephone number so he could find out for himself why they were not going to relieve him of me today. So, that made me feel great – a current host family eager to get rid of me and my next host family not ready for me yet.

(But I know of three families who would gladly take me in straight away, two of which have asked me if I will ask to do so.)

The plan was to leave my stuff here until I get back from the mountains but spend some time with my new host family before I went. But Walenty seemed eager for my stuff to be shifted out of the house – lord only knows why because no-one uses the room. So today I was madly packing my stuff. I felt like I needed a hug but had only a teddy bear. I felt like I needed to pour out my soul to someone but had only a diary. I felt like I needed to cry but had somehow forgotten how to.

It's been a real pain not having my keys these last few days. Miranda took my set when she left. I went to pick up photos, go to the post office and the internet café in the knowledge that Walenty would be home at 3 pm. I got back at 3.30 pm but he wasn't there. I waited 15 minutes. It started to rain and my stomach was providing the thunder. The friends who live closest were all away on holidays. I went to find a phone. I called Tym's house. I explained my problem to his mum and asked if I could go to her house this afternoon. She said 'of course', so off I went. I was greeted with a hug, provided with a comfortable couch to sit on and given sandwiches and tea. The simple things I had missed for so long. When Tym came home he told me about some of his experiences with host families in Australia. It made me feel heaps better. Then he dropped the bombshell. 'When I was camping with my girlfriend.' GIRLFRIEND!!! Since when? Had I read the signs wrongly? How stupid do I feel now? But perhaps I hadn't been in love with him anyway. Maybe it was just lust. Or maybe, in my quest for a bit of love, I desired his gentle and caring manner to be bestowed on me more particularly.

These past few days have been quite an emotional roller-coaster. It's been a challenge to prevent myself from overflowing. It's a shame that it's got to the stage where I can't wait to get out of this family. It's a shame 'cos it spoils what was a great experience in the first few months. It's just these last couple of months that have been very trying. Now that I've got this out of my system I can approach this children's summer camp fresh and with enthusiasm (I hope). Although I won't be all that fresh if I don't go to bed now – I'm leaving in five hours!!!

Tatra Mountains

[Children's Camp]

From: jennifer phelan
Date: Sat, 12 Sep 1998
To: Judith
Subject: AUGUST ADVENTURES

Yes it's me! I'm still alive. You've had to wait a while for this but you won't be disappointed. An epic follows. I've been waiting for my host family to get the internet. Now they do so I should be able to write more regularly from now on. Sit back and enjoy...

AUGUST ADVENTURES: PART ONE

I spent the first 2 weeks of August in the Polish mountains near the Slovakian border as a counsellor for an International camp for children. There were 40 children and 8 nationalities represented. Their ages ranged from 9 to 15. English was the official language of the camp.

There were children from the British school and the American school in Warsaw, many of whom had mixed parentage. Polish children with a good command of English, American children with Polish backgrounds spending the summer in Poland and many other situations. I was one of 4 counsellors. I looked after the youngest but the largest group (12 kids including a pair of identical twins!!) It was the first time I'd done anything like this before and it was challenging but I had an absolutely fabulous time and it is an experience I'll remember forever.

The setting for the camp was a hostel with a pool on the side of a mountain overlooking a deep valley and fir-covered mountains on the opposite side. It was a very active camp and the weather was perfect for all our outdoor activities. In fact, I heard it was the best place to be in Poland during those 2 weeks.

During the first week each group took it in turns to spend a night at a nearby shepherd's hut. It was a great team bonding exercise. Most people chose to sleep outside under the stars around the campfire. The shepherd's hut was basically there just in case it rained (which it did at 3 am and we all dashed for the hut!) Before we settled down to sleep I showed them how to make Aussie damper, which we cooked over the fire on sticks then ate with honey or vegemite.

There were a few half-day and full-day hikes scheduled to surrounding mountains and an opportunity to go mountain-bike riding – two of my favourite activities so I thoroughly enjoyed them. Along the way we would pick and eat wild blueberries, blackberries and raspberries – delicious!

Each morning we had exercises before breakfast. The kids could choose from aerobics, volleyball, soccer or – something new for many of them – relaxation exercises which I introduced to the program. This is something I often did with my Mum during my HSC year, but it was the first time I'd actually lead it. I had a small group each morning and they all said it was great.

Halfway through the camp we had a bus trip to nearby places of interest. It was fascinating for me to see and hear about the mountain culture. We visited a village famous for its crochet garments. We were told about the instruments that shepherds used to use at a former shepherd's house (now a museum). We went to the top of one of the highest mountains in the area for the view – a mountain that has an uncanny ability to pull things up it against the force of gravity! For example our bus driver turned the engine off and the full bus continued to ascend the mountain!! It's a mystery nobody has been able to solve.

We also spent some time in the city of Wisła where Poland's most important river has its beginnings. The river Wisła [Vistula River] flows through Warsaw and into the Baltic Sea at Gdansk (200 kilometres from where I spent the second half of August – but that tale is coming!) In an incredible coincidence, while we were looking around the market square in the city of Wisła, I ran into two of my friends from Warsaw!

One of the activities we did in teams was to prepare a project on an English speaking country. My team, of course, did Australia. We started with an introduction to its geography, people, climate and flag, then the main part of the project was about Australian animals as this topic appealed to them. What I got them to do was to each choose an animal then, from the books I had brought, complete the sentences: 'I live...,' 'I look like...,' 'I eat...,' 'I am...' plus draw a picture to accompany the information. For the presentation we did it like a guessing game – the audience had to guess what the animal was. The first person to do so got a eucalyptus lolly. Once this was completed they got together and sang 'Tie Me Kangaroo Down Sport' which I had taught them. They really got into it and had the audience clapping along with the chorus. To finish with, I passed around vegemite sandwiches while the kids sang, 'We're Happy Little Vegemites'. The looks on their faces when they tasted it was absolutely hilarious and it was all captured on video!

One of the days was an art and craft day. Each counsellor was in charge of a different discipline and the kids could try each one as they pleased. I introduced everyone to Aboriginal painting. I explained the symbols, showed them which colours to use and how to make the dots and left the rest up to their imagination. They came up with some fantastic work and really enjoyed it.

One night we all camped out just down the hill from the hostel. We played a game called totems. The object was to steal the totems of the other teams and protect your own. The totems consisted of a stick and something to identify them by. My team, of course, had the Australian flag as their totem. That same night I gave a slide show of Australia projected onto a sheet outside. It was fun.

We had a mini Olympics day (which actually ran for 2 days). Among the many other activities that took place was boomerang throwing. The kids were enthusiastic about trying out this new sport and I had one girl who managed to get it to return – the little Russian girl from my team who despite her size was incredibly strong.

On the last day I suggested that we play 'Warm Fuzzies' – a game I learnt on Year 11 retreat. Each team member gets an envelope with pieces of paper inside. Within the team we passed the envelopes around and each person had to write good comments in everyone's envelope. You end up (if everyone does it seriously) with a compliment from everyone in the team and you leave the camp feeling good about yourself. It worked. The greatest reward for me was seeing my little negro boy transform from a grumbling, miserable huddle to a beaming, bubble of joy.

Also on the last day we presented the plays that we'd been preparing. My team did a play that I wrote with the help of Lucy (my assisting counsellor – a 16-year-old girl from England). Lucy and I played the roles of children while the kids were counsellors – i.e., a role reversal. We exaggerated everyone's idiosyncrasies – heaps of fun and very amusing. We had a disco on the last night to try and tire the kids so they wouldn't go playing practical jokes during the night. It worked for some but those with endless energy went from room to room putting toothpaste and shaving cream on people's faces while they were sleeping. The fact that we'd confiscated everyone's tubes of toothpaste didn't change anything – the clever ones had squeezed some into a bowl before surrendering their tubes. You see it's a Polish tradition that the last night you spend somewhere is practical joke night. It's called Green night. Thankfully nobody got me as I had set a trap across my door that would wake me if anyone tried to enter.

It was quite sad to leave. After 2 weeks of living together, eating together and doing almost everything together we'd got to know each other pretty well. I made good friends with the other counsellors, particularly the 2 Swedish girls who have invited me to go and stay with them later in the year. It was a fantastic 2 weeks and thoroughly satisfying. The guy who ran the camp gave me a 20% increase on what he was originally going to pay me as he was very pleased with my work and in the book he gave me he had written:

> 'You are a great ambassador of Australia!
> You put lots of life into International camp!
> Your team's project and play were great!!!
> I am really happy you came to Poland and to my camp!'

Podkowa Leśna

15-8-98

I awoke this morning with a feeling of emptiness. No children to go and wake, no cuts and grazes to attend to, no hikes to prepare for. A new house. A new family.

Today I went with my new host father and host sister to collect some letters of mine from the house of another Rotarian. This Rotarian is the secretary of Warsaw Rotary Club and these letters were from my Rotary Club in Australia dating back months. They had been misplaced by mistake and only now discovered. No wonder I had been extremely puzzled as to why I hadn't heard from my Rotary Club. Included was an 18th birthday card signed by everyone and a cheque for $100!!!!

Next we went to watch an international tennis tournament for a little while. At 2 pm we visited my host grandparents, then some friends of the family who have email so I was able to send a quick note to everyone. We ate *obiad* at a well-known fish and chip restaurant. We returned home and I speedily packed for the seaside.

We are now on our way to Agnieszka's house where I will stay the night and at 5 am we'll leave for the Baltic coast.

So, that was my first day with my new host family. I haven't met my host mother yet as she is in Greece at the moment.

Now I feel sick from writing in the car. I have to write on the move as I don't have any other spare time.

Baltic Coast

AUGUST ADVENTURES: PART TWO

From the fresh air of the mountains to the fresh air of the seaside.

The second half of August was spent in quite a different situation. I joined my best friend Agnieszka, her parents, her older sister and their dog for their family holiday by the Baltic Sea. We stayed in a holiday house attached to and owned by the Post Office. It's one of many around Poland especially for Postal workers (like Agnieszka's mother) and their families. I pretended to be their cousin from Australia! It was a modern building in a small town which survives solely on summer tourism. We were just 200 metres from the beach; a beach that reminded me of Main Beach on Wilson's Promontory, Victoria, Australia. Very different from what I had expected. Beautiful soft white sand and a band of trees and shrubs hiding the settlement behind. The Baltic, however, is colder, calmer and not quite as blue as our Pacific Ocean. The weather of the first few days was superb for enjoying this lovely setting. Sunbathing, reading, eating sunflower seeds from the flower and swimming. Every so often a doughnut seller or an ice-cream seller would walk past carrying their eskies and shouting their distinctive cry. It was great to relax after a tiring 2 weeks. It would have been about 30 degrees on the hottest day. The Poles embraced the opportunity to strip off and tan themselves. I was the only one wearing a T-shirt, hat and sunglasses.

Some evenings we went for a walk along the beach and watched the sunset over the sea. Some evenings we took the bikes that came with the house and rode inland along dirt lanes through wheat fields, golden in the evening sun.

Unfortunately the weather turned. Autumn came early. The wind blew up, aggravating the sea, plunging the temperature and bringing rain. But we didn't spend the whole of our time indoors. We went for trips in the car to nearby places of interest. We went west to within 50km of the German border, on territory that was once Germany's until WWII. We saw the ruins of a church precariously balanced on the edge of the eroding coastline that 200 years ago was 2 km from the coast. It reminds me of the holiday with my parents on the south coast of Australia, Christmas 1996, when we drove along the Great Ocean Road and learned of another ocean's influence on the form of another coastline. The fascinating Twelve Apostles being destructively caressed by the foamy blue – a natural monument to the passage of time. Seeing things like this makes you realise just how precious time is.

I really enjoyed being in a family situation again where the itinerary and activities were organised by someone other than myself. I was accepted into the family as another daughter. An additional sister. I shared a room with Agnieszka and in our chats before going to sleep she would tell me fascinating stories about her childhood – growing up in Warsaw in the 80's as the revolution against communism was gaining momentum.

23-8-98

Unlike my host families, Agnieszka's family are fairly devout Catholics. No meat on Fridays, church on Sundays and no work on Sundays. Today is Sunday. After *obiad* we'll go into Kolobrzeg for the service in the cathedral but this morning we're doing nothing. I've taken the opportunity to start my new novel *Poland* by James Michener, or should I say re-start. I began to read it in Australia a couple of months before leaving for Poland, but it was a library book – I had to return it after making only a small advance into its thickness. Reading it again now after living here for 7 months has so much more relevance for me. And I have on hand Agnieszka, a knowledgeable student of Polish history, who I can ask questions when I want something clarified. On our way here we drove through a forest which Agnieszka told me used to be the secret hide-out for 10 thousand members of the Russian army during the occupation. I just read in the novel about this same situation in a forest in southern Poland.

Last night on T.V. I spotted Lech Walesa in the audience of the concert at Sopot – the famous politician known for starting up wharf workers unions. His name was mentioned a few pages back in the novel regarding this very event. I've heard so many stories of the times when there were no products in the shops. This is part of the novel too. And the blackcurrent juice I've tasted, the Vistula River and beech tree forests I know, the thatched cottages and fields of wheat I've seen, they all feature in the book. The novel starts at the beginning of the end of communism in Poland. Soon it will delve deep into history but first it balances on the delicate, tense tightrope of 1981. 17 years on and almost 10 years into democracy here I am experiencing Polish life as it is now, where it is each for his own, not each for his country. Inevitably, democracy has brought materialism and from my experiences the more materialistic someone is the less religious they are.

I prayed in Polish today. I didn't mean to. I started to subconsciously, so I continued. I'm thinking in Polish again. It's taken a week to get back into it after such a long break – 2 months almost.

24-8-98

Last night I watched *Dead Poets Society* on T.V. I love that movie. The part where Neil dies and all the school comes together for the funeral brought back memories of Katherine's funeral at the end of Year 11. My first encounter of death, or should I say loss. I wonder if she's looking down on us from heaven, following the lives of her old school mates as they fractured in so many different directions with the end of school.

It's weird how everything I do or see lately reminds me of something from my past. I turned on the T.V. just now and on the Euro News cable channel was a little feature on the incredible and sudden return to popularity of the yoyo and there was the world yoyo champion who I met in 1996 at the Newcastle Uni design students' exhibition. One of the students had designed a wiz bang yoyo and his wiz bang father had imported the world yoyo champion for the occasion (paid for his air fare from America!) It's nice to see that he still wears his cute little cap on backwards!!

25-8-98

Last night before we went to sleep, Agnieszka and I got talking about religion, Polish history and ultimately her childhood. She told me some fascinating stories. She was born in 1980, two months after me, but in Warsaw where the rumblings of a revolution were getting louder. There was only one maternity hospital working and even though her mum had some birth complications she was sent home without treatment, but not before she almost left with the wrong baby. Even after all she'd been through she was alert enough to realise that the baby the nurses handed her was not her Agnieszka! As Agnieszka grew up during the early 80s it was normal to see tanks and Russian soldiers parked near the apartment blocks. Just watching. Waiting. When you talked on the phone a man's voice would remind you at intervals that your phone call was being monitored. Letters arrived already opened with a red stamp on the envelope signifying it had been read.

When Agnieszka went to primary school she was taught Polish history Russian style, i.e. that it was the Russian army that helped Poland fight against the Germans in WWII. One of the first things that happened after 1989 was that the history books were re-written to tell the truth. The Russians, yes, were there but they didn't help, they just stood by and watched. Waited. Even killed some Polish soldiers too as in Katyń, which I learned about when I was in Kraków the second time on 3rd May and there was the procession through the streets.

The communists hated Catholicism. One suggestion as to the reason why there are much fewer people attending church these days compared with the past is that going to church was a way of showing rebellion against communism. Now they don't need to. Another suggestion is that the main reason for going to church was to ask for freedom – a concrete purpose. It's easy to forget to go and give thanks for the freedom now enjoyed. But for Agnieszka and her family it's not only something they've always done, and will continue doing, but a strong belief in the God who gave them life, freedom, family, holidays, sunshine and happiness, made all the more meaningful by the experience of their opposites.

It's funny but I've noticed that everywhere we go they are judging things according to how they look – what people are wearing, nice street, nice house, nice beach etc. This made me recall what Kylie's host father said in Budapest – that Polish women are thought to be the most beautiful women in the world. I started taking more notice and the conclusion I reached is that they're not necessarily beautiful but they just take a lot of care in how they dress, how they do their hair and wear plenty of make-up and perfume. This concern for appearance would also explain the seriousness with which they tan themselves.

Podkowa Leśna

26-8-98

I returned to Warsaw 2 days earlier than Agnieszka and her family in order to be here for Pip and Simon's arrival. I got the overnight train from Kolobrzeg to Warsaw arriving very early on Thursday morning. My new host father met me at the station and drove me home. We ate breakfast together then he zipped off to work. A few hours later my host mum and sister rose.

I waited for Pip and Simon to call from Kraków to say what train they'd be on, then my role as tour guide began. Unfortunately they didn't have nice weather for their 3 days in Warsaw but it was bearable. I took them up the Palace of Culture for the view of the city, to the Old Town and its museum, to the summer palace and the palace on the water. We also went to visit my old host family and I showed them my old school and where I used to go riding.

Budapest

AUGUST ADVENTURES: PART THREE

I accompanied Pip and Simon, who were visiting from England, on the next leg of their trip – to Budapest. We met up with my Aussie friend Kylie who showed us around her host city for 4 days. Our first day consisted of a bus tour of the city. Great views from the castle on the hill. Day 2 began with a visit to the national museum. It was fascinating to compare Hungary's history with what was happening in Poland at the time. In the afternoon we did the art gallery. We had a great traditional Hungarian meal then took a night-time cruise on the Danube to see the city in lights. We began day 3 with a guided tour of the magnificent gothic parliament building standing symmetrically and stately on the river bank. After this the 4 of us, plus the other Aussie exchange student in Budapest, hired one of those family bike things and explored Margaret Island. In the afternoon we relaxed in one of the city's thermal baths. In the evening I went with Kylie to her Rotary meeting which was pretty similar to the ones in Warsaw. I introduced myself and said a few words about my situation and was able to meet some other exchange students. On our last day we took a trip to the Danube bend where the former capital of Hungary is situated. You can see Slovakia on the other side of the river. I returned to Warsaw by train that night. I had a few hours to shower, eat and repack and then it was off to Torun for the weekend.

Torun

AUGUST ADVENTURES: PART FOUR

Torun is a town 4 hours N.W. of Warsaw where this year's Rotary Exchange Student conference was held. There were a total of 24 students (the total number in Poland) from 7 different cities. The majority were American, one from Canada, four from Brazil and two from Australia (me and Jade). It was great meeting another Aussie. She's from Melbourne, 2 years younger than me. She's staying in a city 4 hours S.W. of Warsaw. Like me she has been here almost 8 months yet it's the first time we've met! We were the odd ones out – everyone else has only just arrived. We suggested they have two conferences a year from now on – holding the other one in February so it benefits the Aussies.

We arrived Friday evening and the first activity was supper within the ruins of the castle of the Teutonic Knights. That was the first opportunity to meet everyone. On Saturday a Rotarian gave us a lecture on Polish history, a local school teacher advised us on how to survive the Polish school system and the Rotaract students went through the Rotary exchange rules with us. Then 2 or 3 people from each country gave a presentation. I found out about it 10 minutes before I had to do it! Thankfully I had brought plenty of resources and with Jade's help we threw together a presentation about our country that consisted of many pictures and ended with a eucalyptus lolly for everyone. In the afternoon we had free time to explore Torun and in the evening everyone was swapping badges and visit cards. On Sunday a professional guide gave us a tour of the city then we said our goodbyes amid promises to visit each other. So now I have met the new exchange students who are living in Warsaw. There are 5 girls from America and one Brazilian boy. Now it's my turn, as the 'oldie', to show them the ropes.

What an incredible summer it's been. As one who desires variety I think I've succeeded here. First to England, then to Italy, then the Polish mountains, then the Polish seaside, then to Budapest and finally Torun. The whole concept of summer vacation has such an explosive atmosphere in Europe. It has been a totally different experience from our 6 weeks of summer holidays in Australia which is broken up by Christmas and New Year. When you finish school in Europe around June 20, two and a half months of uninterrupted summer vacation lie ahead of you. Now they lay behind me but the memories will be forever with me.

Now I'm settling in and getting to know my new host family. I've started at my new school and made some friends there. My old class haven't forgotten me. They've invited me to go with them on their next class trip – to Gdansk at the beginning of October!

Until next time,

Jenniferek (as I am sometimes called by my new host father!)

6-9-98

Oh my! So much has happened in the last 12 days I just feel so numbed by it all. In Torun I overheard some of the American girls talking about some of the guys – who they thought was cute, who they liked etc. I thought back to the briefing weekends in Australia when we used to rip off the inbounds 'cos they were always pairing off. I remember thinking at the time *I wonder if I'll be like that next year?* But no, I really hadn't been bothered with 'checking out the guys' at all. Jade told me that she has a Polish boyfriend and it's a bit difficult. And I thought to myself, as we were walking back to the hotel, *Nah I don't want to start a relationship.* Little did I know how things were to change in the next few hours.

At the hotel everyone got out their badges and business card and started doing the rounds – trading and swapping. I ended up in Daniel's room with the other Brazilians and started looking at his photos. Mysteriously everyone else seemed to leave the room and in his open confident Brazilian way he got me to sit next to him so he could tell me about the photos. Soon he was offering to give me a shoulder massage and still naïve me hadn't noticed his admiration of me, but one thing led to another and basically now you could say we're an item.

After three hours of sleep in my own bed I woke up confused, wondering if it had just all been a dream. My head was a muddle of thoughts. It all happened too quick. This was not meant to happen. This is gonna really muck up relations with the girls now. What am I to do? I found it difficult to face him when I went downstairs. It wasn't until after breakfast that I could look at him.

I was apprehensive about us being seen together in front of everyone else, but gradually I overcame this and we spent most of the tour hand in hand. He's a very intimate person, always putting his arms around me, kissing my head. It's really nice to have a bit of intimacy after sooo long. It was only a few days ago I had been envying a couple on the Budapest metro, so enamoured by one another that a bomb could have gone off next to them and they wouldn't have noticed. But that's the danger and the entire reason why dating is discouraged by Rotary – that you miss out on other things when you have a serious relationship with one person. And I recognise that I was missing parts of the tour as a result. But he's so nice. Let me tell you about him. He's 19 and comes from Curitiba near the coast in southern Brazil. He's got dark blond hair, a goatee, and is slightly taller than me. He's short-sighted. He has a surf tattoo on his left arm. (He loves surfing.) He's just completed 1½ years of journalism at university. His 17-year-old brother is also currently on a Rotary exchange but in Sweden. He's quite funny and loves to talk even though his English is limited. He learned English in school for six years like most Brazilian students, but the English language education is bad apparently, and if you want to learn English you have to have private lessons. He didn't speak English when he arrived three weeks ago (nor Polish) and after this time his English is great. He's in such a difficult situation but his enthusiasm and determination shine through which is admirable. Like me his attitude is to try anything, go anywhere, basically to 'Do it, be it, live it' – unlike what I've experienced of the Americans so far.

It was quite funny 'cos we spent most of the bus journey in each other's arms, but as soon as we arrived in Warsaw to the awaiting parents we had to pretend nothing at all was going on. My host sister Julia even sat between us in the car. It's so ironic. Out of all the exchange students, all those who were trying so hard to get a boyfriend/girlfriend, I who wasn't even trying at all, end up with Daniel, the only pair of the camp (other than a few Rotaract pairs).

Oh, the other thing about Daniel: he has a girlfriend in Brazil!!!!

Podkowa Leśna

I took today at a nice slow pace – something I haven't done for a while. I slept in, had a nice shower and washed my hair, ate breakfast at noon. Put some clothes in the washing machine, sewed some badges on my blazer, wrote a letter to Alex (the next exchange student to Poland from Australia who in fact lives only 15 minutes away from my house in Oz!). I ate *obiad* with my new host mum and Julia, then took a walk to take my films to be developed and my letter to the post office. After this I took a bike ride part of the way with my host mum as she was going to visit a friend. We split and I came back and explored more of Podkowa. I'd hardly been back for half an hour when Daniel came with his host brother (Marysia's brother) and invited me to go around to their place for a while. They were also on bikes so I got the bike out again and went with them. It was the first time I'd met Antoni, as only today he returned from the States where he worked over the summer with a children's camp. He's 20 and really nice. It was funny 'cos when I was riding alone I thought *It's good that Daniel and I are having a day without seeing each other* – then he comes over. Anyway it was a nice evening.

They are such a nice host family in such a nice house. I kinda wish I was living there, but that would mean Daniel wouldn't be, but it would also mean I'd be living with Antoni ☺. We sat and talked around their open fire with music in the background. I helped Daniel with his Polish. He's started an exercise book of words. It transported me back to when I had just arrived in my first host family – my sheets of words, talking about Australia, settling in, new discoveries. Daniel was showing and telling us about Brazil. This same family will be the first host family for the next Aussie exchange student – the one I wrote to today. They had her application forms. I went through it with Ema translating it into Polish for her. Those same questions I remember filling out last year. I was quite amazed that I could translate all but two parts – it was a fun exercise for me. Amid all this, Ema, the beaming, bubbly, motherly lady that she is, was offering food every five minutes. We ate supper together and arranged to travel to Rotary on Wednesday night and to all go to the theatre on Saturday night.

By this time it was 9.15 pm. I called home to say I'd be home in half an hour. My host mother reminded me I have school tomorrow, blah, blah blah! I'd trade in my host mother for Ema any day. It's so different living with my new host family. I feel like I have to justify everything I do, tell all the details of what I've been doing, and that they watch me and talk about me and judge me. Ahhhh! And even things I don't tell them they find out anyway.

It was a lovely evening as I said, but it was a little tense – or rather unsure – between Daniel and me. We didn't get a moment alone and I wasn't about to make any show of affection in front of Ema, Jaroslaw and Antoni. It was obvious Daniel was dying to but the chance never came. Antoni drove me home as it was dark. The bike went in the back of the car so there was no room for Daniel to come with us. He blew kisses from the driveway. In some ways I wish we were just friends, but in others I enjoy being endowed with affection. I guess I should just look at it as another challenge – trying to keep a balance between my love life, my family life and the time I spend with friends – sustaining a relationship without it hindering the other two aspects of my life. An important life challenge I guess.

It was funny, when I got home and was talking with my host mum about who I was with and what we were doing (justifying), she asked me who was more handsome – the Brazilian or the Pole. I answered (I guess to Julia's surprise, as she was within earshot) 'the Pole'. But it's true. Antoni is blonde, blue-eyed, tanned and cute. Daniel is good looking too but in a different way. Don't get me wrong, I like him very much, but it's a case of me being chased not me doing the chasing. I've often thought the fun is in the chasing. In this instance it was Daniel who swept me off my feet and before I knew it I was in the middle of a relationship. I think I'm over the stage of asking myself why a guy would possibly like me, but I'm still unsure of how to act once in a relationship and surrounded by others. I know it can be quite uncomfortable for people when there is a couple in the vicinity. Something to work on.

9-9-98

It's chronic. He's hopelessly in love with me. I love being loved, but do I love him? I'm still trying to figure that out. We didn't see each other at all yesterday. It was my first day at my new school. I was prepared for it to be much worse than Lelewel but it's fine. I'm in class 4C and so far they're really nice. I have two days when I finish at 3.30 pm the others are 12.30 pm. It's quite a modern school in a lovely setting and it's quite big as the classes range from Kinder to 4th class (final year). Today I arrived late because I couldn't work out how to open the gate and therefore missed the train I was meant to catch. I think I did exactly the same thing on my second day at Lelewel!

My family now have the Internet. Yay! I spent all afternoon writing my August epic (four pages) but didn't have time to send it. Antoni and Daniel came for us at about 6 pm and we headed for Rotary. At the last minute my host mother decided to come with us. Daniel wasn't pleased about this as he was expecting that we'd have the back seat to ourselves for the whole journey. Julia sat with us in the back and our mum in the front. We dared to hold hands, and at one stage Janina (my new host mum) looked around and did a double-take. I had to try very hard not to burst out laughing for the rest of the trip. We dropped her off about 10 minutes before our destination. As soon as she was out of the car Daniel told Julia, in no uncertain terms, to sit in the front and then hauled me over close.

All the exchange students apart from Carly were there. (Her host family lives in Austria.) It was the first meeting for Daniel, and Chloe from America, so they had to introduce themselves. Most of us wore our blazers. There was a returned exchange student who gave a little talk, then Julia spoke about the weekend in Torun, and then I spoke about my vacation.

I felt much more comfortable with the American girls tonight. I think we're going to get along OK. I think it was a good idea that I phoned them all individually last night to see how they were going and tell them we'd be going out after Rotary. Speaking to them on a one-to-one basis helped to break the ice a bit. We were talking tonight about their first experiences of school and host families and it took me back to the time I was going through all that, which seems an age ago.

Antoni couldn't drink, of course, 'cos he was driving – unfortunate for him but great for us that we had a lift home. He's a great guy – understanding, generous and fun. On the way home I mentioned to Daniel my travel ideas and we both agreed it would be great to travel together, but that any more would be too difficult. However it would be rude not to invite the others. A difficult problem.

Tomorrow I'm not going to school. Yay. Thank goodness as it's 1 am already. My family are taking me to Łódź for some exhibition or something. We still have to get up at 8 am though. My host mum is getting on my nerves. She just came in to see why I wasn't asleep yet.

11-9-98

'I would love to love you like you do me
I'd love to love you like you do me
There's a pillar in my way you see
I'd love to love you like you do me'
[The Corrs, 'Love to Love You']

This is what I was thinking yesterday but today I know that I'm hopelessly in love with him. I so missed him today. I wrote him a poem which goes like this:

> Eu Te Amo....
> Like an ocean wave you enfold me in your arms
> I love that
> With eyes alive with enthusiasm you tell me of your Brazil
> I love that
> In your sweet romantic way you whisper compliments
> I love that
> With lips as soft as the summer sky, you kiss me
> I love you.

Yesterday was our day trip to Łódź. First stop was one of the palaces owned by a former factory owner. Łódź is an industrial city made up of several factories situated right by the palace of the owner. It was interesting. Within the first half-hour of being

139

home the phone rang four times in a row for me. Firstly Antoni, then Grandma, then Agnieszka, then Pieter. I found it hard to talk to Grandma. She told me Grandpa is not too good and they've backed out of the house move. They also said Mum and Dad are somewhere in the south of England. Dear Agnieszka called to say everything is fine for me to go on the Lelewel school trip to Sopot. I'll be in a room with Sonja and Patrycja. She told me the times and cost and I arranged with her that I'd come and visit Lelewel on Tuesday. It was great to get a call from Pieter whom I haven't spoken to in ages. And so timely. I was going to call him to see if it was going to be possible for us to meet in Żoliborz when I am there on Tuesday. That is all lined up now too.

It's so amazing to have a family who takes me places, buys me things, organises things for me. Having a Rotarian as a host father means, for example, I just have to mention that I haven't received my pocket money from the club for the past three months and then magically 300 zł is slipped into my hand at the Rotary meeting – 75 more than there should have been! Of course it comes with its disadvantages as well – my independence is more restricted now.

But life is still sweet. Sweeter than ever. How fortunate, out of all the host families there are, that Daniel and I end up two streets away from one another. 12 hours till I see him again – I'm counting.

12-9-98

I don't believe this is happening. My host father woke me up at 9 am saying we're going at 10 am to the castle. I have no choice. There go my plans to spend the day with Daniel. I just called to tell him – it hurt. Again I've not had enough sleep, again I have no time to clean up my pigsty, and again I have no time to finish sending my emails. Ohhhh!

13-9-98

Well, yesterday I ended up staying at home. It was a last-minute decision. Five minutes before Josef, Janina and their friend left I decided I was too sick to go. So I stayed home and spent most of the day sending emails – it was satisfying to get that done. I'm glad I did get up early and eat breakfast with the others though because I had a very interesting conversation with Janina's friend, the one who had been staying with us. She is Polish but moved to Chicago during the occupation of Poland and now lives in England. She was visiting for a few days. She was saying how she can hardly sleep here 'cos life is so stimulating in Poland. Things are changing so quickly – in leaps and bounds, while England seems to be stuck in time, not moving anywhere and isolated from what's happening in mainland Europe. Something I can agree with wholeheartedly from my experiences this year and from what my parents have told me. Poland is grasping new technologies, looking to the future, aiming high, while in England if you're lucky enough to find an office with a computer between six people it's bound to be an old one.

Daniel and his host parents came for me at about 6 pm. We saw the ballet *Zorba the Greek*. It was very beautiful with the combination of dancing and a full choir in the wings. The set and costumes were fairly simple but the dancing great. Just before they dropped me home I slipped the poem into Daniel's hand. It became a bit of a game – sneaking a kiss when host parents weren't looking and holding hands under a jacket in the car. But I'm not allowing this relationship to rule my life – I'm still alert to what's happening around me and enjoying the company of others too. After today I find myself falling in love with Antoni so I'm a bit emotionally confused at the moment. If I could have Antoni's head, brains, intelligence, humour and particularly his gorgeous blue eyes and of course his Polishness, with Daniel's body and love for me, I'd have the perfect guy! But things don't work like that.

I spent today with Daniel and his host parents. We went to Częstochowa. I've been twice before but I saw and learnt some new things. The weather was ugly – cold and rainy all day. Beaming, bubbly, motherly Ema had been plying me with vitamin C tablets all day and to go home with she gave me a package of apples, pears and plums and some herbal tablets. She must think my family don't feed me. Already she was making plans for next weekend. Life is sweet.

Before I went out last night my host mother was complaining about the mess in my bedroom, which I knew was bad and needed fixing, but truly I'd had absolutely no time. This morning I did a quick tidy up job before I went (hiding most of it behind the curtain where it can't be seen) and now I'm in her good books again.

'Season of mists and mellow fruitfulness
Close bosom-friend of the maturing sun
Conspiring with him how to load and bless
With fruit the vines that round the thatch eves run.'
[John Keats, 'To Autumn']

I had a chance to sit and observe autumn this morning. Falling leaves and scampering squirrels. And on our way back from Łódź the other day harvest activity was in progress in the farms and an eerie evening mist hung over the land.

'The squirrels' granary is full
And the harvests done.'
[John Keats, 'La Belle Dame sans Merci']

14-9-98

Things are a bit of a mess. I can't write about it at the moment.
I'm thinking about tomorrow – a day I've been looking forward
to for a few days now. I'm off to Lelewel to see my old friends
again then I'm meeting Pieter at my old family's house. I hav-
en't seen him for two months.

16-9-98

Well, things are a bit better. OK, first I'll write about yesterday. It was fantastic. I went to visit Lelewel again. It took me
almost two hours to get there, but it was well worth it. I arrived
at 9.30 am and a busload of students from Israel were visiting.
The same type of trip that visited Lelewel before, when I met
Yael. Anyway, everyone was really glad to see me and likewise
I was ecstatic about seeing them all. I got hugs and kisses from
left, right and centre. We talked about the vacation and I showed
my photos. It's been three months since I've seen most of them.
I sat through their lesson of history and paid for the trip to
Sopot. They were all sad that I'm no longer going to Lelewel but
happy that I'd be joining them for the trip to Sopot.

After school I went to Agnieszka's house where I gave the
skirt to her sister, showed her my photos and Agnieszka made
a tape for me of Polish songs. It's great. Most of them bring
back certain memories of my year. At 4 pm I was at my old
host family's house where I met with Walenty and Pieter. We
chatted and exchanged photos. I picked up a few things I'd left

behind then went to the Old Town where I was expecting to meet Agnieszka – but it didn't work out.

In an incredibly amazing coincidence I met Daniel and Antoni on the train. The amazing thing was not only that it was the same train but that I got on the same carriage, and out of the two vacant seats, chose the one next to Daniel before I'd even realised it was him. It was uncanny. Destiny. I so very nearly got on the first carriage rather than the second, and then very nearly took the closest vacant seat rather than the one next to Daniel. Anyway, Antoni didn't look too happy that evening and no wonder when I found out they'd just spent four hours sending emails – well, Daniel sending emails and Antoni waiting.

So, the problem the other day (Monday) was that I finished school earlier than I expected, so I went to Daniel's place. I guess there's only one Rotary rule – Don't get caught breaking the rules. Well Daniel's host mum walked in on Daniel and I. It's not like we were doing anything. Only sitting close on Antoni's bed while Antoni was doing something at his desk. After this, she called me downstairs for a private chat. With the aid of my dictionary I got the basic drift of what she was on about: she's responsible for us, she knows I'm sensible but she's worried as we're young and she doesn't want anything to happen... She did the right thing, but it made me feel really bad inside 'cos she's such a big-hearted lady who adores me and would do anything for me and I felt I betrayed her. Not only that, I think she had designs for me to fall in love with her son not Daniel. Little do they know that I wish it were that way too.

Anyway, to add to the cringing emotional knot inside me, Daniel told me tonight something that confirmed that Antoni likes me very much. Apparently he always talks about me, especially before he knew Daniel and I were together. And since he realised Daniel and I were together he's been cautioning Daniel not to hurt me. To add insult to a rather injured day, my host parents were not in the happiest of moods when they returned home. They had been out for a special supper as it was my host father's birthday, and they had hoped I would have been with them. I said I'd called twice but nobody had been at home. 'You should have called the mobile', they replied. Oh yeah, I forgot about that. I'm not used to mobiles. So I felt bad about that, and the fact that I didn't know it was my host father's birthday. But how am I supposed to know these things if they don't tell me? So I was feeling very down and wishing Daniel and I had never got together as it had caused agony to at least three people today. As a result I was a little cold towards him yesterday when we met accidentally on the train, and then again today when he came over before Rotary. But tonight things warmed up again. He loves me much more than I love him and he realises this. I'm not proud of it. After a week and a half I've lost enthusiasm for the relationship. It's the kind of substance (in the form of intelligence and humour) that Antoni possesses that would sustain a fun relationship. Oh what a difficult situation I'm in.

19-9-98

Yesterday I was wishing I could erase the past two weeks and start over but today things are looking brighter. Yesterday was the first time I'd cried in six months. The last time I cried was in March after that telephone call from Grandma. The cause of the upset this time was as much myself as my host mother. I had been arranging to get a group together to go to Planeta but I'd kind of left the planning till the last minute. It was a very stressful day – helping exchange students get ISIC cards [student discount cards] only to find that they didn't have *legitimacja's* [ID cards] yet, then speaking in front of 100-200 scientists from all over the world at a Promni concert. But before all this I was trying to find somewhere to stay for the night so the night out at Planeta would be possible. Antoni and Daniel were going to stay at their apartment in Żoliborz so I asked if I could stay there too. They agreed, but my host mum was not too keen on the idea and a 40-minute serious discussion ensued. It began with this topic and my inadequate planning, then developed into a monologue about all the things she doesn't like about me. She even suggested I talk with my counsellor if I'm not happy staying with them and see if I can change host family. But it ended with the mutual understanding that she cares about me as her own daughter and can't have separate rules for Julia and me. Meanwhile a flurry of emotions was turning inside me and I couldn't find the voice to express them rationally. Finally I did, saying that I'm not discontent living with them and I fully understand her point of view, it's just that I'm upset with myself for not planning properly because usually I'm good at planning things.

Not a good way to begin my stay with my second host family but I think it cleared things up a bit and we understand each other better now. I've learned that, unlike with my old family who didn't want to know my plans too far in advance, with this family every detail of future plans must be discussed well in advance.

The agony was worth it. We had a great time at Planeta. We stayed in the flat and there were no problems. Daniel and Antoni slept in one room and I in another. Daniel waited till Antoni was asleep then crept into my room. It was nice to be close in the dark and I'm proud that I stood my ground and did not let him have sex with me. This is a topic of great cultural difference between Brazil and what I am used to. He didn't think that I was a virgin.

22-9-98

Today I had one of those moments where you look at your situation and realise how happy you are. I was riding along by a lake in the beautiful Polish countryside as the sun was setting and Daniel riding alongside me. I know I'm in love now. He gave me a beautiful letter today which he wrote at 3.30 am a couple of nights ago. He really wants to go to Australia or for me to go to Brazil so we can be together.

Our bike ride was part of an afternoon spent with Antoni's uncle and family who live in (or close to) Lomianki. It was lovely. We all started out rather nervously polite (Antoni hadn't been there in at least a year) but by the time we left we were all great friends and expressed our mutual wish to get together again some time. Antoni's uncle has a gorgeous little girl and a son Jakub aged 17 who is a brilliant pianist. His wife made us a wonderful meal (four courses) of some of my favourite Polish food. After this we went on the bike ride then we had a concert from Jakub on the piano. He played mostly Chopin pieces. After this we had a photo session and sipped beer. Of course the great feeling of happiness couldn't last. There was a phone call from Daniel's host mother who had spoken with my rather nervous and worried host mother, so when I got home I had another talking to. The problem wasn't that I was returning late (she knew who I was with and that I'd be home some time in the evening) but rather that I'd taken the bike without asking. But the situation was thus: I didn't know we'd be needing bikes until I met Antoni and Daniel this afternoon. When we went around to pick up the bike I'm used to riding, nobody was home, and therefore nobody to ask. So I left a note saying I'd taken it. As it turns out the bike was needed by Julia this afternoon, but luckily she was able to use her boyfriend's as he had left it there yesterday.

Anyway, I managed to convince her that it wasn't my fault and she realised I had done the best I could in the situation.

This evening there were a rare few moments when everyone was sitting at the table at the same time so I seized the chance to give them my Aussie gifts. They were very appreciative and seem happier now.

It was beautiful weather today – cool but sunny. The TV and radio were giving conflicting information about whether this weather will last. One says today was the last of the good weather but the other says we can expect the same tomorrow. I hope for the latter as it's great weather for photography and I'd like to take some photos of my new house and new school.

I went to school this morning but couldn't find my class. When I asked a teacher where they were he told me they have their trial *Matura* exams today. Nobody told me this yesterday. So I went home and on the way thought about how much I miss Agnieszka and realised how lucky I was to have her as she always kept me informed about what was going on at Lelewel. I want to make something really nice for her but I'm not sure what yet. So instead of school I went to play tennis with my sister and her friend. I hadn't played in at least a year. My technique was a bit lacking but I enjoyed it.

The night before last (Sunday) I was with Julia at a party of her old class from high school. They are now preparing for the *Matura* but of course Julia passed her final exams in the States [as an exchange student] so is a year ahead. The party was held not far from here on a property in the forest with a little cottage and a clearing for a campfire. It was fun. There was beer, sausages, bread and sauce and some very interesting people to talk to. Their class teacher was there for a while but when she left we made a fire and sat around it talking and singing campfire songs. I love these types of parties and they're very popular among my age group in Poland at present.

Sunday began with church where I met Daniel's host parents. Afterwards Daniel came back to my place as there was a chance my host father would take us to Kazimierz, but this plan changed as the group of exchange students from Bidgoszez were in Warsaw for the weekend, so we met them in town and took them around. I assumed the role of tour guide as I knew Warsaw better than my host sister! We showed them around the Old Town then we went to Łazienki Park for a while. After this we went to drink beer at a pub and then they had to leave. Daniel and I went to the Chopin concert in the park and met the American exchange girls there. The sun was shining and I had Daniel as my backrest as we sat on the grass and listened to the music. Very pleasant.

23-9-98

Autumn is very pretty, especially here in Podkowa Leśna as we are surrounded by forest – falling golden leaves. The other day my sister and I were raking the leaves from the front garden. When we were walking in Łazienki the other day, I looked up and saw a leaf falling towards me – circling as it glided down. I reached out my hands and ran around in circles determined to catch it. The others thought I was mad. I'm pressing it between two books and will keep it as a reminder of that day. Simple things but I write a lot about seasonal observations because it's something we don't experience in Australia. I didn't write about how I was hit on the head by a falling chestnut the other day. Yeah, it's true. I walked under a chestnut tree and one got me right on the top of my head with such force it brought tears to my eyes.

Well, my parents will be in Singapore now. I spoke to them on the phone the other night before they were due to fly out of England. It was great to talk to them again. They said I was speaking English with a Polish accent. Of course I didn't say anything about the problems I'm having with my host family – no need to worry them. I painted the picture of perfection. I guess it's about time I had a few problems as, other than the incident with moving out of my previous host family, it's been a dream eight months. I can't believe I've lived in Poland for eight months. I'm really sad I've got only four months left – there's so much more I want to do, but at the same time I'm kind of mentally preparing myself for returning home – thinking about my house, my friends and what uni life is going to be like.

I'm at the stage now where I'm very passionate about the fact that I'm Australian. I realised this yesterday. Antoni was explaining to his cousin that I was born in England but moved to Australia when I was three. A little to my surprise I rather firmly said, 'But I'm Australian not English.' It's rather weird because for many years when we first moved to Australia I clung to my Englishness and refused to become an Australian citizen. By the time 1989 came around and my parents decided it was time we got citizenship I was at the stage where it didn't make much difference to me – I felt half English, half Australian and realised that taking Australian citizenship didn't mean I was rejecting my English heritage.

I remember very vividly the day, the moment, when something happened inside me to create such an overwhelming emotional patriotic feeling and I thought to myself *I am Australian and I love my country.* It was about two years ago. I would have been in Year 11. It was around the time my friend Lana left Australia and moved to live in Texas. I was on a bike ride with Mum, Dad and Auntie Judith in Sydney. The destination of our route was the

oldest Presbyterian Church in Australia – a small stone building near a river. I stood on a tree stump and looked out over the
Australian landscape, and that's when it hit me. Tears came to
my eyes and when Mum asked me what was wrong I couldn't
find my voice. It was a very strange feeling. I remember emailing
Lana in Texas soon after this as she was very sad and not settling
in well. I remember writing something like, 'for a long time you'll
cling to your Australianness and feel like a foreigner in your new
land, but one day it will hit you and you'll call Texas home'.

'I've been around the world a couple of times or maybe more
I've seen the sights I've had delights on every foreign shore
But when my friends all ask me the place that I adore
I tell them right away
Give me a home among the gum trees,
With lots of plum trees,
A sheep or two and a kangaroo
A clothesline out the back
Verandah out the front
And an old rocking chair.'
[John Williamson, 'Home Among the Gum Trees']

24-9-98

My love for Daniel goes up and down like the waves, like my
moods. Yesterday I was depressed during the afternoon but he
was happy. We were in Warsaw and met with a friend of his who
he had met in Karwice. By the time the evening came and we
went to Rotary my negative energy had transferred to him and
I was feeling better. But today we clicked and were close. He's
such a sensitive guy and says some beautiful things but I can't
help being wary. It's very hard to express what I want to say. I've

constructed a kind of imaginary barrier. My love for him is very deep but not entirely sure. This barrier represents this small per cent of unsureness. I feel I can talk to him about anything. It was weird but today we were having a conversation about periods. It was so strange to be talking about this with a guy!

After school we met and went to Żoliborz to visit Agnieszka who is sick. I took her a card and punnet of raspberries. After this I went to visit Agata and Walenty and showed Agata my photos as she wasn't there when I visited last week. Of course I told them the truth, that I miss living with them and liked Lelewel heaps better than my current school. It was so lovely to sit and chat and joke with Agata. We were laughing at least once every ten minutes. I really love her and I told her so, and that I've been having problems with my new host mother. But as I said to Agnieszka and Daniel today, it's all part of the exchange experience: learning to adapt to different lifestyles, and learning to live peacefully with people you may not necessarily get on with. Today, not only did my host mother tell me off about the mess in my room in front of Daniel, but also made such a big deal out of it when all she needed to say was, 'Can you hurry up and tidy your room please?' She even threatened to ground me if it isn't done by tomorrow – it sounds so childish. I've never even been grounded by my own parents!

26-9-98

With friends and in the company of important people, my host mother shows me off proudly, but at home she does nothing but complain. I killed them with kindness today. I bought the bread and prepared breakfast, presenting it nicely on the table as I knew my host mother (being an artist) appreciates this type of thing. She was very pleased. The problem with having host siblings is that you're forever compared, so whenever I do something good it makes Julia look bad, and whenever she does something good I look bad.

We spent the day today on the property of the richest guy in Poland (also a Rotarian) who had a huge name-day celebration. He lives only 10 minutes from us. It's the same place where we had the farewell party for the last lot of Brazilians. He has a beautiful old wooden house, a gorgeously landscaped garden surrounding it with pergola, swimming pool, waterfall and tennis court. Also on the property is an extensive set of stables, horses and plenty of surrounding fields to ride through. On arrival there were some refreshments then the 400 or so guests boarded horse-drawn carts of which there were about 20. About 30 guests were dressed in traditional hunting clothes and rode ahead on horseback (a couple even in the old-style Polish costume). One of these men had a fox tail attached to his shoulder. I was on a cart with the other exchange students (Daniel, Cindy, Chloe and Brooke).

The party of 20 carts paraded along narrow sandy tracks through the forest in its autumn splendour pursued by camera crews from National TV stations. There were two stops on the way in two large fields where the race to catch the fox's tail took place. All riders had to chase the guy with the fox tail on his shoulder while the remaining guests looked on and helped themselves to the drinks that came around. We arrived back at about 3 pm for a huge banquet in the garden. Fortunately the weather was beautiful making it so much more enjoyable. There were tables stacked with all sorts of salads and breads and meats. Huge pots of *bigos* [stew], *zurek* [soup] and *kiełbasa* [sausage] on the grill, plus beer, vodka and an abundance of fruit juice. Several waiters were to-ing and fro-ing dressed in black and white and a musical duo (accordion and keyboard) provided the music. Daniel and I both agreed that we felt kind of out of place as guests at this type of function. We felt as though we should have been serving food or washing dishes or something. There were very important people present – actors, politicians, etc. One guy had even arrived in his helicopter.

Us exchange students tended to stick together for most of the day. After we'd eaten we found a nice spot on the grass behind a clump of trees and lounged around. From time to time I went to sit with my host family. My host mother was drunk – quite funny. Daniel brought several letters that he hadn't read yet and sat reading them. He began to cry. It was a letter from his grandparents that triggered it. He's close to them and they were saying how much they miss him and he's worried they will die before he returns. Then with every subsequent letter fresh tears appeared. It was quite strange for a 19-year-old guy to cry, but I thought it was so sweet and I comforted him the best I could. He's certainly a popular guy. So many letters, so many emails. With every day I love him more and realise how hard it's going to be to leave. He's an amazing guy – he only made the decision to come on exchange 20 days before he flew out of Brazil. He took the place of the guy who was originally coming but dropped out. And he's got such a responsibility to try and mend the bad reputation of Brazilian exchange students. I think I've found a way to describe that barrier I was talking about in my last entry. It's the barrier of time. I know that the more I allow myself to love him the harder it's going to be to leave.

He'll be starting uni soon – Journalism in Polish. I wonder how he'll cope. I talked with Rotarian Maksym today about the possibility of me attending uni – architecture, as I explained that I've already finished school in Australia and have a place to study architecture when I return, so it's rather senseless attending high school. I hope something will work out as I'm not too keen on my school here in Komorow.

Well, my parents will be back in Australia now. I checked my email tonight but nothing as yet. Perhaps they'll call tomorrow. Daniel and I were talking with Maksym and his wife for a few moments at the party today and one of the topics was missing parents and friends. Daniel was saying how he misses family and friends a lot but not in the way that it makes him want to go home. At this moment I felt like I wasn't an exchange student. I felt like I was a Rotarian or just a Pole looking on, listening to the plight of exchange students, because for me it's not the case. It makes me feel so cold-hearted when I say I don't, and never have during the year, missed my parents and friends. Sure I think about them often and look forward to seeing them but I don't miss them or cry over a letter from them. This has been one thing that has surprised me about myself. I always was very emotional and certainly I'm very close to my parents. But as I think I've said before, the love between my parents and me is the kind where we can love each other from a distance knowing that we'll see each other again soon.

I'm not cold-hearted at all. I'm a very loving person. When the love in my heart can't be bestowed on those it is normally bestowed on, I find new people to love.

27-9-98

There's a kind of anxious atmosphere in Poland at the moment. Everyone is eager to make full use of the good weather as any day soon the full force of winter will be upon us. We spent today at the house of our new exchange student Chairman, Wicek, in Konstancin. It's a property to take your breath away. Gorgeous white house almost like a palace surrounded by fantastically landscaped grounds, a tennis court, pergola thingy and outdoor eating area with BBQ. There's an indoor pool under the house with its own sauna, massage parlour, bar, disco lights and pink piano. The house is furnished with expensive modern furniture, wooden floors and many paintings. There's even a resident maid. This guy is rich! His son is currently on exchange for a year in California, and one of the new exchange students is going to live here! Towards the end of the day, us exchange students plus some Rotarians got together in Wicek's office and had a chat. They were really nice – saying things like they hope this year is going to be a great experience for us, and that we take every opportunity, and that if we have any problems don't hesitate to talk with any of them, and that we should organise trips for ourselves, and talk with them and they will help with the arrangements etc etc. It made me so mad that all this is happening for the new exchange students. I had nothing like this when I arrived. I voiced my opinion and asked that they consider doing something like this in January when the next Australian arrives. It was the same scenario as the Torun weekend. Us Aussies are always left out as we're 'upside down'.

I was over at Daniel's tonight as my host parents were out at a concert and I didn't have a key. Ema told me that she had spoken with my host mother on the phone today (for one hour) and my host mother had said that she doesn't like me spending time with them. Neither of us understands why. I can't believe this woman. Of course I didn't mention it tonight when they got back, but gee it makes me mad. I wish I were living with Ema and Jaroslaw!!

28-9-98

I've never been so in love! The more I love him though, the more aware I become of the fact that I'm leaving in 15 weeks (so Ron delightfully reminded me in his email yesterday).

1-10-98

Things are good – family life, love life. The relationship between me and my host mother is much improved. I know how to deal with her now. We've been talking a lot lately and she likes me more now. I've realised that it's nice to have a family who is interested to know every detail about everything I'm doing. I got too used to living with Agata and Walenty who were not overly interested. My real parents fit in somewhere between – they're very interested in my happenings but not overly so.

A good balance.

Meanwhile Daniel and I love each other more than ever. We have so much fun together and whenever we're in each other's company we're always striving to be as close as possible. It's as if we were made for each other. We had many happy moments today. During one of them I happened to mention that I have only 15 weeks left. This made Daniel depressed for a few minutes. But I told him he's not allowed to get depressed when I leave – he's got to go on and finish his exchange and have fun. It's so weird, we've known each other for just over three weeks but it seems like three years. If you think about it mathematically that's one-sixth of the potential time we have together here in Poland. I say potential as I intend to spend another one-sixth on a trip which he is unable to come on due to a financial crisis in Brazil. He told me today that now that he has met me he regrets his past because I am so pure and he feels so dirty! You know, the way I see it, from my observations – Brazilians are overly party animals, Americans are underly so, and Australians are nicely in the middle.

A good balance.

After Rotary yesterday, Chloe, Daniel and I went for beer and Chloe said something that has made me feel great inside. We had been talking about Promni; she had been asking how I had got involved and that she'd like to come along one day. She said, 'You're my role model, everything you get involved in I want to be involved in too.' I've often thanked God for inspirational people – Aung San Su Chi, my mother, Andrew Denton, Caroline Corr, Gaudi, Leonardo Da Vinci, Michael Palin, Agnieszka, and the list goes on. It's so nice to know that I am now an inspiration to someone else.

I met with Mariusz before Rotary yesterday and talked business – I'm going to be teaching two English classes for an hour each, two times a week, earning about $300 a month. He is keen for me to do this. He said he interviewed 20 Polish people for this but chose only four. It'll be another challenge but one I'm looking forward to. Afterwards we went to meet Gizela, his girlfriend, and went for coffee. She'd just been to her German lessons, then spoke to me in English while driving through the centre of Warsaw in a small Fiat. Quite a feat! (ha ha.) Mariusz is in the process of finding a job in marketing. We talked a bit about business and the opportunities in Poland right now. With such a fast pace of change, ways of thinking become redundant very quickly so it's the young people with the new knowledge who get the jobs.

I read something very interesting and rather ironic in my *Lonely Planet* guide today:

'Eastern Europe has been the source of much of what we know as western culture.'

Yet it is a region now trying to become like the west.

Sopot

The class trip to Sopot is great so far (apart from the cold), though I feel a little awkward as I'd like to spend the time with my friends but they're always leaving Daniel and me alone. Yesterday we went to Gdynia. I thought I was going to die from the cold. We had a tour of a WWII fighter ship then in our free time Daniel and I walked to the end of the wharf, got some lunch and did some shopping – I bought a sweater and scarf. Last night we went to the movies here in Sopot to see *The Horse Whisperers.* We were in such a happy light mood before it, which came plummeting down with this sad and rather long movie. It was good though. I could identify with the mother character. There was one line that really appealed to me. I don't remember exactly what it was but the idea was that for some people the 'feeling at home' feeling is an inside feeling rather than dependent on the outside surroundings.

Later...

'Half of my heart doesn't want to share you with anyone else, but the other half wants you to have fun and be happy because I love you.'

This is what Daniel just said to me! We had been discussing our inevitable separation and the idea of an open relationship.

Later...

We spent the day in Gdansk today, the ancient port city where *Solidarność* [Solidarity] had its beginnings. It wasn't quite as impressive as I had been expecting. We walked along Dlugi Targ with its beautiful old buildings (like Warsaw, rebuilt after the war) and the Neptune monument. We visited the largest brick church in Europe and went to the top of its tower for the view (405 steps). We walked (a long way) to see the monument to the shipyard workers. Later we went to Westerplatte, the site of the beginning of WWII. There is a monument and a large sign saying:

> *Nigdy Wiecej Wojny*
> (No More Wars)

7-10-98

Our last morning in Sopot was very special. A memory I'll treasure forever. Daniel and I walked barefoot the length of the beach. It was cold but the sun was shining and there were very few people. Part way we stopped and sat under a tree. We held each other and listened to the waves and watched them rolling onto the shore and felt the fresh breeze on our faces. A very special moment. We found a double shell still joined. We held a half each between finger and thumb and lightly pulled. The halves separated and we vowed to keep our half shells forever.

I left something very special in Sopot – my virginity. They say if you leave something in a place you'll return one day. He's not angelic but I think he was sent from heaven. He was so sensitive and sweet. Even after all his experience he was more nervous than I was. He tells me at least 20 times a day that he loves me. He says it in English and I say it in Portuguese.

So far in Portuguese I can say 'I love you', 'I want you' and 'Give me a kiss'!!

Early in the year I was writing about what I look for in a guy. I wrote that one of the most important criteria is that I like myself (how I am) when I'm with the guy. This is certainly fulfilled with Daniel. We have so much fun together. We're like Siamese twins – always together but we rarely (never yet) get sick of one another. Almost all of the other characteristics I wrote at that time fit too – humorous, intelligent, romantic, adventurous and that something special – twinkling amber eyes and an undying love for me.

Daniel proposed to me tonight!! I told him I'd give him my answer in two years' time!!

Podkowa Leśna

Back to the reality of a capital city.

It's a little harder to hold back twinges of homesickness at the moment as the three elements that contribute to homesickness are in the ratio that provokes it. My parents and my home are together again, and my family life here is not too enjoyable.

We spent the day at another of these picnic-with-horses things. There were about 50 guests at this party. We boarded horse-drawn carts and rode through the forest to a monument. This monument stands for the South African pilots who had been flying in supplies to Warsaw civilians during the war, but were shot down by Germans and landed in this forest. The exchange students and I placed a floral wreath on the monument. We continued on our journey. Daniel was quiet all the way. We arrived at a spot in the forest where a fire had been prepared. We ate *bigos* and cooked *kiełbasa* over the fire. On the way back we went fast. It was heaps of fun but Daniel almost fell off and was not amused. He told me he didn't feel comfortable at these types of things. He obviously needed to talk, so when we arrived back at the house we went for a walk behind the house and sat on a low tree branch. He told me how a lot of things have compounded to make him feel bad. To top it all off, on our way back two large black Rottweilers charged at us. I managed to run away, but Daniel was bitten on the arm. It was so quick I hadn't realised what happened until he took his jacket off and revealed a nasty bite mark. I was so lucky – it so nearly could have been me. I took him straight over to where the people were gathered and said what had happened. I couldn't believe how nonchalant everyone was. Nobody seemed to care. One lady took him to get some ice but there was no apology or anything. They told us it was our fault for going behind the house – but how were we to know that firstly, we shouldn't go there and secondly, that there were dogs there? This tipped the balance for Daniel and he had to struggle very hard not to cry.

12-10-98

'We are so young now
We are so young, so young now
And when tomorrow comes, we will just do it all again.'
[The Corrs, 'So Young']

Pip and Simon sent me The Corrs tape which I've been listening to all day. As I opened the gate on my way out a package fell in front of me. It had been placed atop the gate as it was too thick to fit in the mailbox. Inside was the tape plus a letter and photo. I read the letter on my way to Warsaw. I laughed at the part where Simon wrote he was devastated that I was no longer available for marriage – joking of course!

I bought some black trousers at the markets under the Palace of Culture then went to meet Daniel. Together we went to visit Agnieszka who is back home after 15 days in hospital with pneumonia. We told her all about the trip, showed photos and I got her to sign my Lelewel T-shirt. I gave her the present I had made her. The decorated Frugo bottle. Inside were the glass stones I collected on the beach in England. The bottle itself came from Gdynia. On the lid I stuck Australian flag stickers and the waratah. Around the bottle I attached a ribbon featuring the Sydney Opera House and Harbour Bridge. It was joined with my 'J' stamp. So, all in all, it was quite a totem. Something to represent my country, my state, my state capital, me, my past and my year in Poland.

Yesterday I went with Daniel and his host family to Żelazowa Wola, the birthplace of Chopin. First we stopped by Żoliborz as they had to vote in local elections. We arrived in Żelazowa about midday. We visited the humble white home where Chopin was born. It's now a museum and during the summer months, concerts take place there every Sunday. We had a guided tour of the house in English which was very interesting. Then we walked around the lovely gardens which surround the house – particularly beautiful with their autumn colours.

We ate at a nearby restaurant serving delicious Polish food. On our way back to Podkowa Leśna we passed through the village where Jaroslaw grew up, and visited the church where he ministered for a while. It was built by St. Maximillian, the guy who gave his life in Auschwitz to save another man. This church is the second most important Catholic pilgrimage site in Poland after Częstochowa. It's an interesting '20s building and we watched a small historical animation there too.

15-10-98

The Corrs quote with which I began my last entry illustrates well my life at present. While hectic, fast-paced, full of happenings and potentially stressful, I'm keeping calm, patient, focussed and having heaps of fun. Recently I've realised a big change in me – I don't worry half as much as I used to. I remember the many times last year I'd burst into tears over an assignment or something, and Mum in her skilled way would

say things like, 'Well what's the worst thing that could happen?' These days I'm doing things like teaching three classes of
English with no previous teaching experience, attending architecture lectures in Polish, and walking in the centre of Warsaw
at 1 am with NO WORRIES MATE!

Well, actually, the last example was an accident, and yes I
was rather scared. It was Wednesday night. Since the weekend
I'd been calling people and organising to go out to Ground Zero
after Rotary. After all the people I'd called, there ended up being
only four of us. Midweek is not so convenient for most people.
Nevertheless we had a great time. I had arranged to sleep at
Alina's house and Daniel was going back to a friend's place. In
the end, unfortunately, Alina couldn't come with us as she had
to visit her grandmother in hospital, but she said Danika (her
sister) would meet us there later and we'd return home together.

For an hour or so before going to the club we went to a pub on
the way where I met an exchange student (1995) to Poland from
America who now lives in Poland. She was fascinating to talk
to. I met her previously at the Rotary picnic in May. Hearing
the stories of her experiences and where she is now was very
inspirational. It helped me to see the big picture again. I realised
that lately I had been buried in nitty-gritty things due to the
influence of the other exchange students. That's what I appreciated about Jake – we'd talk about the world, life and philosoph-
ical questions. With the new exchange students I find my set
talking about day-to-day problems and that's all. This American
girl (whose name escapes me at present) speaks fluent Polish,
has been working in the American consulate in Kraków and now
finds herself being pleaded with by Warsaw Rotary to stay and
study in Warsaw, all expenses paid. I hope I can leave half as
good an impression as she obviously left.

Ground Zero is a cool place – underground. Wednesday night is student night – only 8 zł and unsurprisingly it was very popular. So popular that at 11–12 pm it was impossible to find Danika. I was not too worried – I was having too much fun dancing with Daniel. I even danced on one of the block things for a while. Then Daniel and his friend left. A wave of fear came over me – I lost my confidence. I continued looking for Danika for a further half-hour but soon gave up realising it was hopeless, and decided to go back to her house. It was really close, but it was in the centre of Warsaw in an area known for prostitutes, and 1 am, and yes, I walked there alone! I didn't mention this to my host parents. Nothing happened. I was fine – perhaps lucky.

Alina and Danika live in such a small apartment – I hadn't realised how small before. So much so that their parents went to sleep at their grandmother's place to make room for me. But apparently they're used to this when the girls have guests. This was the permanent arrangement while Fiona lived with them. It looks something like this:

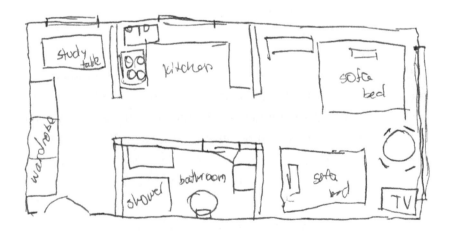

It's interesting to experience how different Polish people live.

I had a leisurely morning on Thursday. Alina and I talked quite a bit, never having to revert to English. I was proud. It's at times like these I think *wow, I'm fluent,* but then I sit through a lecture about architecture not understanding anything as it's all technical vocabulary and think, *No, I'm hopeless.* One thing I've realised is that fluency is not a switch. You can't one day wake up and you can speak Polish. Learning a language is a gradual and ongoing process.

At noon on Thursday I met Karol the architect at the *politechnika.* He introduced me to the lecturers and wrote down for me the classes I can attend. I went to my first one that same day – Elementary *Projektowane* [EP]. He talked for half an hour making illustrations on the board then showed slides for another half an hour. I'll be attending this type of class two times a week and drawing two times a week. So my weekly plan is quite a varied one at present:

Mondays:- drawing
Tuesdays:- EP
Wednesdays:- Polish, English, Rotary
Thursdays:- drawing, EP, Promni
Fridays:- Polish, English

I had to stand on a very crowded train into Warsaw this morning. Then I was fined on the tram as I'd forgotten to punch my ticket. It was so annoying – I'd bought the ticket only two minutes previously. It wasn't as if I was trying to cheat the system. I can't believe I forgot to punch the stupid thing. And I didn't have the time or the energy to talk my way out of it so I reluctantly slammed 49 zł into his hand and got on the next tram.

South East Poland

From: jennifer phelan
19 October 1998
[Fax to K Phelan at work]

Hello.

I've just got back from a weekend in South-Eastern Poland with the other
exchange students. It was my idea and Rotary gave us each 150 złoty for
the trip and organised Rotarians to be our guides in each of the places. First
place was Zamosc, a beautiful old planned and fortified city built 400 years
ago. Three of the girls and Daniel got the bus there Friday afternoon. Brooke
and I went in the evening as we were teaching in the afternoon. We arrived
at midnight after a very bumpy bus ride. I nearly didn't make it to Zamosc
that night because at one of the short stops we made along the way I went
quickly to the toilet, and when I came out the bus was not in the place it had
been. I looked to the street and there it was rolling down the street. I ran
after it terribly worried. Thankfully Brooke, with her limited Polish, managed
to get the message across that I was coming and the bus stopped. I don't
know what I would have done if I'd been left there in the middle of nowhere
on a cold, dark night without my coat, my belongings, nothing! Anyway, I
was lucky. In Zamosc the daughter of one of the Rotarians met us and drove
us to our hotel, situated on the main square.

In the morning the Rotarians had organised a guide who took us around the
city, eagerly telling us its history and some fascinating legends. We visited
the museum, the cathedral and even went into some of the underground

passages that link the gates of the city. After lunch a Rotarian took us
for a drive to nearby places of interest such as the summer palace of the
Zamoyski family who built and owned Zamosc. The countryside in this area
of Poland is the prettiest I've seen. At that time of day (just as the sun was
setting) and this time of year (when the autumn colours are at their most
vibrant) I think we saw it at its best.

Sunday (today) we were taken by minibus to Majdanek concentration
camp – the second largest in Europe after Auschwitz. Again the weather
was appropriately dull and drizzly. Again a harrowingly powerful experience.
This time I had friends to share the experience with – to discuss feelings and
ideas. After this we were taken to a tourist attraction just outside Lublin. It
was a traditional Polish country village, as they were 200 years ago. There
were people dressed in traditional costume performing traditional domestic
chores. We were able to see the interiors of the cottages and in one of
them – a tiny one – the lady told us that 17 people would have lived in it. I
was translating what she said for the others. Funnily enough the weather
changed at this point. It became bright and sunny to match the happy
atmosphere of this village. We'd been taken from one emotional extreme to
the other and the weather mirrored this appropriately.

In Lublin we were met by two guys from Lublin Rotaract. They took us for
lunch then for a quick walk around the old town. Unfortunately we didn't
have a great deal of time in Lublin as we had to get a train back to Warsaw.
It's a university city and hence a large population of young people, and
its old town (not so destroyed as Warsaw during the war) is quite pretty.
We stood squashed together on an overcrowded train for the 3-hour train
journey back to Warsaw so you can imagine how tired I am now. But – as
we said – it was all part of the adventure. It was a great weekend and we
had heaps of fun together.

Next weekend I'm going to Austria with a Rotarian and my host sister. He lives half his time there and is hosting Carly, one of the American girls who will be staying there until the end of the year.

Life is good. Good friends, gorgeous boyfriend and family life is great. Not a day goes by where I don't think about how much time I have left and how I don't want to leave. I love you both very much and I hope you'll fix email soon 'cos I'm really eager to hear from you.

Lots of xxxxxx and 00000000 and ☺☺☺☺☺☺

Jennifer

Austria

From: jennifer phelan
Date: 27 Oct 1998
To: Mum and Dad
Subject: Austria

I've just read your emails and now I'll tell you about Austria. It was awesome. I stayed with a Polish family who live in a gorgeous 2-storey house on the outskirts of the small town of Klagenfurt which nestles at the base of the Austrian Alps. Picture this: in the foreground a lush green lawn lined with colourful flower beds, in the middle distance a band of alpine trees at the height of their autumn brilliance – gold, red, green, amber – then rising majestically behind that the amazing alps themselves capped with pristine white snow! That's the view from their living room window.

It's an interesting situation. Mr Nowak is a Warsaw Rotarian and works in Warsaw too, but he returns to his house and family in Austria for weekends. His daughter Elena is in America on exchange. She's the one who wrote to me earlier in the year requesting some information about Australia for a school essay. They are hosting one of the American girls, Carly. She's happy there with her family and the beautiful setting but there's nothing to do there and she misses being able to do things with the other exchange students. She was the most logical choice for that family because she speaks German.

My host sister was originally going to come with us but at the last minute changed her mind deciding to stay and participate in a horse competition on Saturday. So it was Mr Nowak and I in his large comfortable Volvo. It was a great feeling rolling down the Warsaw to Katowice highway listening to the Corrs, talking in Polish. It was good to have a concentrated 12 hours of speaking Polish. The journey was a bit like driving from Sydney to Melbourne in terms of distance, but we crossed two country borders whereas in Australia you cross one state border.

I learned all about Mr Nowak's family history and kept him alert with the scent of eucalyptus which I had on a handkerchief. He's married to Beata who was born in Gdansk. They moved to Austria soon after their first child, Elena, was born. There are two sons also, one 16 and one 12. They were both born in Austria and have grown up speaking Polish at home and German at school. It's really funny to hear them speak Polish with a German accent.

Occasionally Mr Nowak would call someone on his mobile. His elder son Oskar called from Dublin where he was on a school trip. They were just about to get the plane back to Austria. The airport is 1½ hrs from their house. In freakily good timing we met at the airport. Plane from Dublin and car from Warsaw meet in Graz within 10 minutes of one another.

So over the weekend they were speaking to me in Polish and to Carly in German, then Carly and I would confer in English to make sure we'd understood the same thing.

When we'd just passed the Czech/Austria border we stopped at a service station for petrol and I went to the toilet. I came out smiling after the experience. Lights come on as you walk in, not only is there toilet paper but it's soft, and after washing my hands at the very clean basin the hand towel was also controlled by a sensor, disappearing after I stepped away. You forget what Poland lacks until you travel west.

On Saturday morning Mr Nowak took Carly and me around the town of Klagenfurt – a city currently bidding for the 2006 winter Olympics. It's a really pretty, clean town with narrow tree-lined streets, many arcades and beautiful window displays in the shops. We had lunch of Polish *bigos* and Italian lasagne then went for a drive around the countryside visiting churches and castles and lookouts. In the evening we sat around the fire and showed photos.

On Sunday we all went hiking in the mountains. Halfway up we had an autumn leaf fight and at the top a snowball fight. We had soup in a hut at the top of the mountain. In the evening the elder son Oskar took Carly and me to a pub in town. He's only 16 but can drink because the legal drinking age in Austria is 16.

On Monday I should have been at uni but mountain biking in the Austrian Alps was a little more exciting I think!

Mr Nowak and I said our goodbyes and departed at 6 pm, arriving in Warsaw at 6 am this morning. I was able to sleep during the drive but Mr Nowak, who drove non-stop, after dropping me off, was going to his flat in the centre of Warsaw where he'd catch a couple of hours sleep then go to work. People live hard and fast in Europe. I guess I've adapted to that lifestyle. My host mother has trouble keeping up with my goings-on.

Unfortunately we weren't able to visit Vienna but they've invited me to spend Christmas with them and promised to take me to Vienna if I come. I'd love to as it will be a traditional Polish celebration, but in the magnificent setting of the white Austrian Alps, with the opportunity to go skiing. I never expected, back in April when I received and acted upon a request from Mr Nowak's daughter for some information on Aborigines for a school essay, what benefits would eventuate for me.

So that's my Austrian story.

It's great to be emailing you again and hearing your stories from Oz. I hope you had a nice time in Port Stephens Mummy.

All my love

Jennifer

Podkowa Leśna

27-10-98

Here I am back in Warsaw. We arrived about 6 am and I've had a quiet, slow-paced, home-based day, most of which was spent writing emails.

Daniel shaved his beard off today and gave it to me! It was good to see him again and everything is good now. I was a little nervous about seeing him again as when I left for Austria we were not on good terms. Our first fight. I didn't write about it because I was putting it out of my mind and concentrating on enjoying my time in Austria. I also needed some time to think. Four days apart was good for us. We still love each other. He told me he missed me but not in a bad way – just that he was thinking about me. I guess it was the same with me – I didn't really miss him but it dawned on me a few moments ago that perhaps it's like the way I feel about my parents – we love each other very much and are comfortable at a distance.

30-10-98

'All the world's a stage
And all the men and women merely players'
[Shakespeare, *As You Like It*]

That's how I've felt this week as I go about my life and everyone else going about their lives, and how those lives cross and interact.

I've felt a bit stressed this past couple of days, particularly today. For the first time I'm beginning to look forward to going home. Probably a combination of recent news from home reminding me of the environment (e.g. a poetic letter from my mum about her walk in the bush) and the recent weather here – cold, wet, dark, the streets a mush of soggy fallen leaves. I can identify a few stressors:

* Anxiousness about leaving 'unfinished business' when I return home. What I mean is not concluding my exchange to my satisfaction, such as a visit to Stockholm, Amsterdam and Berlin.

* Fear of time unoccupied. What I mean here is that I feel I must have every hour, every minute planned doing something specific, and when a plan falls through and I find myself unoccupied, I'm anxiously searching for something to fill that spot.

* Meanwhile the other stressor is being the in-betweener mixed up in a problem between Daniel and his host mum, but I'll get to that later.

'There are stars directing our fate
We're praying it's not too late
We know we're falling from grace.'
[Robbie Williams, 'Millennium']

A small voice reminiscent of my grandmother is telling me, *You're young, don't worry about trying to see and do everything, you've got a long life ahead of you.* But I don't think like this. In any case how can you predict when your life will end. I might be dead tomorrow. Time is very precious. If I can live my whole life thinking each day, *If I die tomorrow I'll still be satisfied in what I achieved during my life*, then I think I will have reached the ultimate achievement.

After quite a heavy day today, what with Polish lessons, teaching English and between that trying to organise this weekend and next, I find myself acting as a bilingual counsellor between Daniel and his host mother. Apparently Daniel has done something to upset his host mother but he doesn't know what he did. She thinks he knows but hasn't the courage to admit it and she's not relenting until he admits. She won't tell me what it is either. I want to be able to help, to get to the bottom of this problem because I love both of them and can see both points of view, and can't bear to see such unhappiness and tension. All the characteristics making this home such a pleasure to visit have turned. That happy, warm family atmosphere has disintegrated into a tense, cold, divided one. I don't enjoy spending time there anymore. But there's nothing I can do to rectify the problem. I was just a shoulder to cry on, literally. Polish tears, Brazilian tears, on an Australian shoulder.

1-11-98

Well, this weekend I'm doing something rare. Spending it at home with my host family. It's Halloween weekend, or more properly – All Saints Day and All Souls Day. It's a big tradition in Poland. Everyone takes flowers and candles to the graves of all their deceased relatives. My host father made the journey to Lublin on Friday to visit the graves of his family. Today my host mum will be going to hers which are not far from where we live. Last night we went to the oldest cemetery in Europe as they wanted to show me how it looks with all the candles and flowers. Unfortunately there weren't as many as we'd expected. Most people must be going today so we'll go again this evening to see what it looks like. There was TV filming gear set up to film today's activities.

I talked to my family about the *Catch-22* situation between Daniel and his host mother. Being Polish I thought they might have a better idea of what Daniel can do. They suggested he buy her flowers and apologise for what he did, pretending he knows. So yesterday morning while Julia had her horse-riding training I rode over to Daniel's place and took him to buy some flowers, then helped him write a card. His host parents were out visiting cemeteries and would be until evening. I'm going to call him soon and see how it went. The only problem would be if she asks him to tell her what it was he did, and he still doesn't know, and it makes her even angrier. Plan B was prepared for this situation. A letter Daniel wrote explaining that he honestly doesn't know but he's sorry and wants everything to be good.

We had quite a late breakfast yesterday. It was after Janina returned from taking Julia to horse training so it was just the 3 of us. We began at 11.30 am and stayed talking until 12.30 pm. They were doing the most talking though. I'd enjoy talking to them but they leave no gaps and it's impossible to butt in. I'm only given a chance to talk when a direct question is addressed to me. One of those yesterday was, 'Do you give flowers to your mum to patch things up after a problem?' I had to think for a while and my answer was, 'We don't have problems.' I realised I live with best friends not parents. I missed my best friends yesterday.

5-11-98

It's funny how one good event can throw all the other recent mediocre things into a new light, making life, in general, seem so much better. I saw Tym at Rotary last night for the first time in two months. He called Tuesday night to apologise for not being there last week as he had said he would, and to say that he'd definitely somehow get there tomorrow. I waited and waited. I was bored sitting there with the other exchange students. It was already almost 8 pm and I'd given up hope that Tym was coming. I was just saying to the others that I'll kill him, when he walked in the room, wet and out of breath. My reaction was a little more enthusiastic than perhaps I intended, but I couldn't help it. I gasped, jumped up, threw my arms around him and kissed him on the cheek. I got a chair for him and when I sat down I realised my hands were shaking. The last time I'd seen him was when I was still in love with him. I remember the occasion vividly. It was when Pip and Simon were in Warsaw and I took them out to the pub with a group of my older friends, including Tym and his girlfriend. I wonder if he's still going out with her. This was all before I even knew Daniel existed. I'm starting to realise love is not simple. For example, you don't marry someone because you love them. I love Daniel but I don't think I could marry him. I could marry Tym. He had some great news – he's coming to Australia next summer (Australian winter). I wonder how things might be now if I hadn't got out of the car so hurriedly all those months ago. One can only wonder. But I don't have any regrets.

So we sat down and we talked about his past few months of hibernation, working as a translator in the Polish Parliament. These last few weeks he's been involved in the Third International Conference of Human Rights, working 20 hours a day.

They even paid for him to stay at the hotel next door to the Parliament. He had some great stories to tell about his interactions with world-famous people. He was saying how he'd be at cocktail parties unable to eat or drink and having to translate a social conversation between important people which gradually became more difficult as they got more and more drunk and began slurring their words.

I was just about to show him my recent photos when the meeting finished and my host father came to say 'We're going.' *Szkoda!* [Too bad!] Tym was genuinely disappointed. That's what I love about him, amid all this notoriety and busy life he doesn't forget me, wants to see me and keep up with what I've been doing. He's invited me to his 21st birthday party next Friday and his uni ball the night after that. It will be great fun. I'd felt recently that I'd become undone from Polish happenings as I've been isolated from the friendships in Żoliborz that I'd spent six months developing, haven't made friends at *politechnika* yet, and thus am spending most of my time with other exchange students. Now I feel I'm getting back on track.

I'm writing this on the train to Gdansk. I'm going to Stockholm. Daniel is with me. It feels kind of weird writing like this about Tym when Daniel is sitting right opposite me.

Stockholm

From: jennifer phelan
Date: Wed, 11 Nov 1998
To: group email
Subject: Stockholm

Hey! What's up? I just spent 4 fun days in Stockholm. It's beautiful, grand, cultural and clean with many bridges and lots of water. The weather was perfect – cold (0 to 4 degrees) but clear, sunny with a light covering of snow.

We arrived Friday afternoon and my friends from summer camp Klara and Caitlin were there to meet us. Klara is half Polish half Swedish, and it was with her family that we stayed. She's actually my boss's girlfriend's cousin! They're lovely hospitable people and made our stay very enjoyable. Klara was our tour guide taking us around her city and telling us things we would never have heard if we'd been by ourselves. Her father took our baggage home while we got a tour of the old town by night. We had coffee in an underground café that was once the city's prison!

Saturday we began by meeting Daniel's brother who is on exchange in Sweden. We saw some of the old town by day including the German church and the palace. At noon there was an elaborate 'Changing of the Guards' ceremony at the palace involving about 100 soldiers. It was very impressive – the horn player especially, who made all his notes with no stops. (I mean no buttons, not non-stop.) After this we visited the medieval museum situated under one of Stockholm's bridges. Here we learned of the Viking history. We spent the afternoon in the Skansen – a Swedish theme park with houses from different parts of Sweden, traditional crafts and even some animals. We were lucky enough to see the bears before they hibernated for the winter. From the high side of the park was a great view of the city from where we watched the sunset (at 3.30 pm!!) In the evening we intended to go out to a live music club but discovered that for most places you must be over 20 or over 23 to get in.

On Sunday we went to the Vasa museum, built around the 16th-century ship that sank in Stockholm harbour on its maiden voyage and was recovered 300 years later. Nearby was the Pippi Longstocking museum which was our next visit. We became children again for an hour and journeyed through the world of Swedish fairy tales. Both were very impressive, entertaining, interesting and well presented.

Monday was our final day. We began with a walk around Klara's neat and pretty neighbourhood. We looked in at the local church which has Viking rune stones set into the outer walls. We did some shopping in Stockholm and admired the shop window displays of Swedish design. To finish our stay we went ice-skating on the open-air rink in Kings Gardens. It was the first time for Daniel and his brother. They were funny to watch but they got the hang of it quite well. Also amusing was Daniel's reaction to seeing snow for the first time in his life. On our bus ride from the port to the centre of Stockholm we passed through lightly snow-covered landscape and Daniel couldn't bear being on the inside of the bus. We stopped briefly at a service station and he jumped out to touch it. I guess within the next few days it will be snowing here in Warsaw.

On our way to Gdansk from Warsaw on Thursday we managed to have a 2 hour stop to visit Malbork Castle – the enormous 13th-century red brick construction that was the headquarters of the Teutonic Knights. It was a dream come true to visit this place as I had read about its history in James Michener's *Poland*. We didn't have time for a guided tour but we had fun exploring the place ourselves. Without a guide it's not possible to visit many of the rooms – theoretically! But we discovered that while they lock the entrances, they leave the exits open so we sneaked in the exits and saw the same as everyone else, just backwards.

We had been debating whether to visit Malbork on the way there or on the way back. I'm glad we did it on the way there because Daniel did not return with me. We arrived in Gdansk yesterday morning, got off the ferry and were one of the first in line at passport control. Mine was fine but unbeknown to Daniel his visa specified that he could only enter and exit Poland once. They put him back on the ferry to Stockholm where he will have to go to the Polish embassy, fix his visa and then he'll be let back into Poland. It will be a learning experience for him and a test of personal strength.

Today is Independence Day in Poland. A public holiday. We've just been watching on TV the ceremonies that are occurring in Warsaw. Lots of important people such as presidents from Hungary, Ukraine, Belarus, and plenty of marching men in uniform.

I have only 2 months left now. I leave Poland on the 14th of January, spend a night in London and arrive in Sydney on the evening of the 16th.

Love and best wishes

Jennifer

Podkowa Leśna

A few weeks ago Daniel showed us a magazine which had a table showing the average age in many countries around the world when young people first have sex. Interestingly enough I'm on par with the age for Poland – 18.3 years, rather than Australia which is about 17.

I saw a brilliant play tonight in a small theatre in the Old Town. It was performed by three British actors and was entitled *Art*. The simple setting, use of props and movement were great but the brilliance was in the script. It was the timely culmination of a topic that has been tossing around in my head lately – the conflict between emotion and rational thought. One line really touched me. It went something like this:

'Nothing beautiful was ever born out of rational thinking.'

It went straight to the heart of the problem between Daniel and I. I wouldn't say it's a problem but anyway it was the main substance of our heart-to-heart in Stockholm that I now feel ready to write about. According to him I think too much. I am too aware of the fact that I'm leaving in two months and therefore don't allow myself to fall in love with him. That's the difference. I love him but I'm not in love with him. Daniel on the other hand is so much emotionally involved that our conversation even brought him to tears. It makes me feel so cold-hearted when really I'm not. By the fact that I'm trying to write about it rationally kind of proves Daniel's point for him. But then again it could be argued that writing is art and therefore born out of emotion and romanticism. When I look back on it, this has been a yearlong debate for me. I remember that night in Granada, Spain when Jake and I were sitting out on the square enjoying a rum and coke and talking about life. Or was it the square in Bordeaux as we sat enjoying the afternoon sun and watching the world go by? Anyway, we were discussing whether our characters were romantic or practical. Without hesitation Jake said he was a romantic. I had to think a little, and in the end conceded I was somewhere in between. That is probably why I chose architecture as a career as it embraces both the artistic and the practical. In the course of events I think that unfortunately I've lost some of my romanticism and become more practical.

I've been thinking more frequently lately that I wanna go home. I'm not unhappy and neither am I homesick, I think I've just almost had enough. Had enough of the dull wet weather, had enough of eating alone, had enough of the 40-minute train ride, had enough of trying to learn Polish grammar, had enough of slow computers, had enough of wearing heaps of clothes.

I know I should be trying harder to make friends in my group at the *politechnika* but I've run out of enthusiasm. I lack the energy to pursue a friendship when I have only two months remaining. I know in this situation it could be beneficial for my future, for example, if I ever wanted to do a uni exchange and study architecture in Poland for six months or so.

I got word today that Daniel has his visa and is returning on the ferry, which means he should be home tomorrow night. Someone else who comes home tomorrow night is Alojzy from Australia. This time for good. Mum and Dad collected him from school after his final exam a few days ago and gave him some things to bring me. But unfortunately I will be unable to meet either Daniel or Alojzy because I'm going to a university ball with Tym. Well at least I hope I am as we are yet to figure out how I am to get home at 3 am. It should be fun though. His girlfriend will be there also. (He is still going out with her!)

15-11-98

SNIEG! SNIEG!! SNIEG!!!

IT'S SNOWING! IT'S SNOWING!! IT'S SNOWING!!!

All heavy thoughts seem to have been lifted by this delicate, white, powdery stuff which has transformed what was a dark, dull world into a brighter, lighter one. It's amazing what effect snow can have. It's a cool feeling when snowflakes fall in your eyelashes, and to catch them on your tongue, and to feel them crunch under your feet. Late afternoon was when it started.

This evening we've been ice-skating at the indoor rink in Warsaw. That is me, Daniel (safely back from Stockholm), Julia, Brooke, Chloe, Cindy, Mariusz and Gizela. Alojzy (safely back from Australia) and Pieter were there also but didn't stay to skate. It was great to see him. He wants his jacket back, unfortunately. I love that jacket. I really don't want to have to buy one for two months. Anyway, I got my hug from Mum and Dad that came via Alojzy. And we confirmed the fact that I'd go to their place for *obiad* tomorrow.

So, I'll be an only child for a week. Julia is packing for a week's trip to Zakopane with her class. I'll be able to sleep without the radio on. I'll have to bear Janina's monologues alone. You know, I wrote the other day how I've had enough of eating alone. Eating together as a family is just as bad. There's always an argument between Julia and her mum about her portion. Janina always wants to give her more than she wants. There's usually an argument between Janina and Josef during the course of the meal in voices far too loud for dinner-table closeness. Then Janina is always the last to finish because she insists on telling me a long story on something. Meanwhile I sit watching her food go cold and wondering how long it's going to take for her to finish.

On Saturday evening my host parents went to see a film while I was at the ball and they collected me at 1 am. The ball was not really a ball but rather a disco. I'm glad I didn't buy a dress for the occasion. Even in my LBD [little black dress] with a blouse underneath, I was a little overdressed. Most people were in jeans and shirts. There were a lot of people. There were two rooms – one with the bar and a few tables, the other for dancing. The thing I like about 'home-made' discos is that they play a variety of music 'cos they want to please everyone. So there was some techno, some rock, some pop, some heavy metal, some slow numbers etc. It especially pleases people like me who like a variety. I had fun dancing with people I didn't know but I didn't care. I danced a slow one with Tym when his girlfriend was out of the room. He really knows how to torment me though. Being so charming toward me one minute then all over his girlfriend the next. This was the second time I'd met her and this time I got to know her a little better. She is very nice (and very lucky!!)

But seeing Daniel again today made me realise that I'm lucky too. I can be myself with him. With Tym, I feel I'm not good enough and hence feel a little timid.

16-11-98

OK. The novelty of snow has worn off. It's bloody cold! Some Aussie sunshine would be welcome. Especially since I've now had to return Alojzy's coat to him. I now get around in two thinner coats, one mine and one borrowed from my host father.

As I was searching for an address I came across a little bookmark Mum had slipped in my folder. It read:

> 'Things turn out the best for those who make
> the best of the way things turn out.'

Rather timely. I'd been thinking today that it looks like I won't be getting to Amsterdam as this weekend is the only time I could fit it in. And then new plans began to materialise such as an invitation for *obiad* with Agnieszka and her family on Sunday, and an idea that Martyna might come to Podkowa on Saturday, and that Saturday night I may be able to go to the theatre with my old host sister.

This all eventuated from spending the day in Żoliborz. I spent three hours with my old class, showed them my photos and caught up on news. My article had appeared in the school magazine in my absence and I've been asked to write a summing up article of my exchange year for the next edition.

I slept without the radio on last night for the first time in ages and it was really difficult to sleep! I've got used to it now and I think I sleep better if it's on.

19-11-98

One thing I love about snow is its undiscriminating nature. It covers everything until the world appears as house-shaped

snow, car-shaped snow, tree-shaped snow. And the way it spar-
kles. It's been constantly snowing light, fine snow for the past
few days. Unfortunately it's not the right type for snowmen
though. It's now -12°C.

It is good snow for sledding though, which we plan to do this
weekend using the trays we stole from McDonalds today.

21-11-98

On Thursday after drawing class I went with Daniel to some
Brazilian friends of his for lunch. We ate rice, beans, cutlets and
salad. It was either that or something I ate earlier that made me
terribly sick with diarrhoea and vomiting that night. I woke at
4 am with awful stomach pains. I felt like I needed to be sick
but I couldn't. One minute I was cold and shivery, the next hot
and sweaty. I looked in the mirror and was shocked. I looked like
a ghost. Not me at all. I was returning to my room but fainted in
the hallway. I don't know how long I was there but when I came
round I went back into the bathroom and made myself sick by
sticking my fingers down my throat. I felt much better. I went
back up to my room and got my diarrhoea pills and Gastrolyte
tablets, then went back to bed. I felt better in the morning,
just tired from interrupted sleep. I thought I could make it OK
through the day so off I went to get the train to Polish lessons.
It's at times like this I really miss my Mum. I had a little private
cry on the way to Warsaw.

After Polish I met Daniel and we went to eat. I shouldn't have
eaten. It made me feel sick again. I almost gave up and went
home but I didn't, I gathered myself together and pressed on.

Daniel came with me to work as my guest speaker. It wasn't
too difficult taking the classes because two of them had tests. I
had to run out of one to be sick in the toilet but luckily Daniel

was there to look after them.

After lessons, we went to the movies with Mariusz and Gizela to see *Lulu on the Bridge*. It's a very symbolic film with no answers – it leaves you to figure it out for yourself. Very interesting though.

The movie was a convenient dark place to have another cry and then when I got home I cried non-stop for about an hour by myself in the kitchen, then went to bed. I knew that part of it was PMS. But it was my first real feeling of homesickness. The situation here was upsetting with the cold, feeling sick and alone and meanwhile thinking of my parents at home going for bike-rides, having BBQ's, relaxing in the spa, going for walks on the beach.

But I'm feeling much better this morning. I got an email from Dad and sent a long one to them about this week. Now I'm going to meet Daniel and we're going to Cindy's for the afternoon. When I called Daniel, Antoni answered the phone. He asked how I was feeling – if I was better today. Quite ironic. My family knows nothing about my being sick but Daniel's family does.

23-11-98

I never got to Cindy's on Saturday. My immune system (I call them my soldiers) had been so busy fighting off that virus that they didn't see the little flu buggers coming! After walking to Daniel's and breathing in cold air for 15 minutes it hit me, and I ended up staying at Daniel's place for the day. I lay in his bed and he made me soup and told me stories. He left for his Brazilian party at 6 pm and Antoni drove me home soon after.

I spent Sunday moping around the house in my PJs. I think it was the worst day of my exchange. At breakfast I was totally ignored. I think they didn't believe I was sick. I wasn't really hungry. I was deciding what to put on my second slice of bread. My host father asked me what I wanted and started to pass the meat. I asked for the jam and my host sister passed it over. Then in ultimate rudeness, my host mother says to my host father, 'Couldn't she get it for herself?' Being as fragile as I was it didn't take much to make me cry so I began to cry. I turned and stared out the window for quite some time, then went back to bed.

Things are better today though. I'm feeling better physically and emotionally. I gave uni a miss and had another PJ day. A parcel arrived from my parents. It was a present for my host parents. I presented it to them this evening when everyone was together for *obiad*. They were very pleased.

I'm rather afraid of leaving the house after two days without putting even a finger outside. I heard on the radio today that 36 Polish people have died from the recent cold – half from drinking too much alcohol in an attempt to keep warm.

52 days left. That means 54 days until I'm home. As I wrote in my emails today, I'm torn between the joy of returning home to family, friends, warm weather and all that means home, and the disappointment of having to leave behind the friends and country and everything that has been a part of my exchange experience. And that is what it has been – an experience, not just a year of fun in another country – you can do that as a tourist. The timing was very important towards this experience too. Doing it while I'm young but not too young. I would call it the modern world's version of the ancient tribal initiation ceremony. I'm being initiated into adulthood.

25-11-98

A month 'till Christmas.

I've returned to health and happiness. As my host mother said in Polish tonight, 'When you experience the bad times it makes the good times so much better.' That's just what John Keats was on about in his 'Ode on Melancholy'.

Today was good. Back in the swing of things. I turn up to Polish lessons and guess what the theme of today's lesson was? The flu – talking about symptoms, medication, visiting the doctor, etc. After the lesson I went for a walk in the park nearby. The barren trees cast long shadows across the snow-covered ground, even at midday. I came within two metres of a tiny scampering red squirrel.

I ate at the bar on Pl. Trzech Krzyzy. I had *barszsz* [beetroot soup] followed by pork cutlet with potatoes and cabbage salad. Terribly Polish. Oh, and of course, tea. I sat for a while in the warm environment reading my book (James Michener's *Poland*). I'm now up to 'The Terror' of WWII; cringing at the cruelty and utterly inhumane way in which the Poles were treated by the Germans. I glanced up for no apparent reason, other than to rest my eyes for a few seconds, and caught an elderly lady looking at me. She was sitting at the next table, just finished her meal. She smiled. I smiled back and returned my eyes to the text. The words blurred together as I wondered what was she doing at the time when the Nazis were subjecting the Poles to such fear and harsh labour. Was she a farmer's daughter, who watched as their centuries-old family quern [hand mill] was wantonly smashed to pieces to put an end to the production of home-made bread?

Then it was off to teaching. With all my layers of clothing only my eyes were showing. I was wearing a jacket borrowed from Daniel's host mum. It seemed to give me more authority.

As I walked in the gate I passed a group of boys who immediately stopped their mucking about and said, 'Dzien dobry [good afternoon].' I hadn't said anything!

The lesson went well today. I was pleased. I gave assessments back to two of the groups. It's irritating when your most annoying, least attentive student attains the highest mark in the class and your favourite student, who always tries her best, gets the lowest mark. That was the case with my first group. It was heartbreaking to see Caroline's disappointment and drop in enthusiasm when I gave her the test.

The Rotary meeting was very pleasing too. We had a lot of laughs as we discussed experiences and I remembered similar things that happened to me that are now happening to the others. I talked with Mr Nowak. I like him so much. He's such a joker and an expert in alcohol but he's so easy to understand, always has a special hello and a smile for me. We finalised arrangements for our trip to Austria for Christmas. He's going to take me for a day in Vienna en route!

I also talked with Maksym about the possibility of spending a few days in Karwica before I leave because I've never been there. 'Of course,' he said. 'It's tradition that the Aussie exchange students have their farewell party in Karwica. It's already arranged for the first weekend after New Year.' I jumped for joy.

There was much talk about Thanksgiving. The American girls are putting on a do for all exchange students, host families and selected Rotarians tomorrow night. I'm looking forward to it even though it means I have to miss Promni.

26-11-98

I've just finished washing my hair in the sink. I have to go three days without a shower because the wastewater tank is full and won't be emptied until tomorrow.

The Thanksgiving dinner that the girls put on tonight was a great success. I didn't eat much all day then pigged out in the evening. I'm used to eating at Polish times so I was very hungry by the time 6 pm came. I'm going to have to get out of the habit of eating at Polish times soon as I'll be going back to where we, too, eat our main meal in the evening.

The girls did a great job with the food. Everyone was so inquisitive and cautious about it but once they tasted it they liked it (all but the pumpkin pie that is). I had to repeat so many times that I'm not American, I'm Australian, this isn't my tradition, as so many of them started asking me questions about the customs or the food. It was a great occasion culturally and socially as it brought most of the host families and other important Rotarians together, so it was an extra opportunity for the adults to discuss Christmas arrangements and future trips. Maksym said that there are places enough for 12 for the weekend in Karwica – my farewell party. So, there's the seven of us exchange students (Carly should be back from Austria) and then I guess Tym, Alina, Alojzy, Pieter and one more. Oh, my sister of course.

The others all found out their second host families tonight. Some are happy, some not. Chloe is unhappy as she's staying with our chairman who lives way out of Warsaw.

My departure date feels so much closer now that I don't have any free time until I leave – everything is planned (kind of). And the fact that people are beginning to ask me, 'Are you sad that you're leaving Poland soon?'

27-11-98

Ahhhh! I'd forgotten how good soap and water feels on the body. Three days without a shower makes you realise how much you take this daily privilege for granted.

Had quite a busy day today. I overslept my alarm but amazingly was out of the house 15 minutes after getting out of bed and managed to get the train. Ironically the theme of today's Polish lesson was insomnia. A strange thing just happened. I couldn't remember that word in English but knew the Polish word and used my Polish–English dictionary to translate from Polish back to English to write my diary!

After class I met the other exchange students. I dragged them along to help me set up the books for my brainchild – the Warsaw Rotary Exchange Student Library. Yes, today marks the official beginning. A small beginning with ten books but my vision is that when I return to Poland some years down the track it will have grown to be quite a healthy collection and a well-used one. It is housed in the Warsaw Rotary office, which is situated a floor above my host father's office in the centre of the city behind the Marriot Hotel. A handy central place but unfortunately only accessible during the hours of 9 am and 4 pm. However this is the only possibility. Cindy was the first to write in the book (which I hope will be covered in International stickers when I'm here next) as she became the first borrower. Everyone thinks it's a great idea. Daniel said he was really proud of me and my imaginative ideas.

29-11-98

Today I made *obiad* for my host family. In the morning I found out that my host grandparents were coming too which made me nervous as they are rather critical people and traditional in their tastes. However, everybody thoroughly enjoyed the stir fry and rice I made for them – it was a great success. Josef said he's going to buy a wok and I must teach them how to make it.

I found an old Polish coin in the snow the other day. Being printed in 1990 doesn't constitute being old, but it's old in the sense that those of its kind are no longer used. It's a 100 zł coin. In 1994, due to the high rate of inflation, they dropped four zeros off and hence this coin is really only worth one groszy.

30-11-98

The last day of November. *Dzien Andrzejki.* The Polish equivalent of St Valentine's Day. Daniel and I learnt of the traditions and customs surrounding this special day through Gizela who is into keeping cultural traditions alive. We had a fantastic evening with her and Mariusz. We met at 5.30 pm after her German classes and went to a pub on Nowy Swiat for hot wine and we played some of the games there. First one was with a bowl of water. On small strips of paper Gizela and I wrote boys' names and then hung them around the rim of the bowl. Each of us then took turns to place in the centre of the water the small paper boat that Gizela had made, and we all waited to see which name the boat touched first. That was to be your future husband. The guys did it too with girls' names. None of us got who we wanted but it was fun and we laughed a lot.

The next game made use of the cups we'd just finished drinking from. We made a strip of paper look like a ring, another to symbolise a baby, and to symbolise bachelorhood/spinsterhood we used a burnt and broken match. Each was placed under a cup. One person mixed them and then one person chose one. Both Gizela and I chose the ring and therefore, as the superstition goes, we will be married within the next year! Daniel will have a baby and Mariusz will be a bachelor!

At 8 pm we met a friend of Gizela and together we went to Pub Lolek situated in a park in Mokotów. A traditional style Polish pub that was throwing a big party for this special day. Upon entrance we were given a party hat and a number on a sticker by guards in fancy dress. The band was good and every so often there was some kind of game or contest. The only dampener to the evening was having to call our host parents to ask permission to stay an extra hour and therefore get home at 11.30 pm rather than 10.30 pm. Luckily that was OK with my host father but when I spoke to Daniel's host mum, I got an ear-bashing about how unsafe it is and that this is the last time. From now on Daniel must be at home by 10.30 pm every night. I tried to explain to her how we were experiencing a unique and interesting Polish tradition but she wasn't happy, even though she begrudgingly agreed.

Nevertheless we enjoyed it. Daniel expressed to me tonight more than ever before how much he loves me. His major goal is to come to Australia as soon as possible. The more special moments we have like this, the more special they become. He told me, 'When I come to Australia, I'll be cigarette-free and speak perfect English.' I assured him that I not only love him but I'm in love with him.

I got a package from Australia today. Some Aussie carol tapes and CDs plus some Billy Tea and other food items. A bag of gum leaves from our garden, a newspaper article and a little poem were also included.

1-12-98

Why does it happen so often that an emotional high must be followed by an emotional downer? Around the breakfast table this morning many things came out in the open, including a fresh batch of tears. It all began as a result of me asking whether such a rule existed that host families must know exactly where their exchange student is at all times, and the address and phone number and when they'll be back. I was asking on behalf of Daniel, and I explained that Daniel's host mum had not been very happy when I called her last night. 'Neither were we,' my host mother assured me, then launched into a major attack, the basic message of which was that I am too busy and don't spend enough time at home talking with my host family. I'm too independent and energetic, leaving home early and returning late. Then came the emotional blackmail.

'I don't know what your parents are like, maybe they don't care about you, but we want to treat you as our own daughter, and we hoped you would have become close to Julia but no... You treat us like a hotel, here only to eat, shower and sleep. And you know you are lucky that you're with us as we've agreed that you may attend the Polytechnika when really you should be going to school in Komorow every day and coming straight home. We've agreed that you may teach, even though we know it's against the law because you don't have a working visa. You know we're only doing this because it's your last couple of months here.' Then she proceeded saying 'And you never tell us about what you're doing or about Australia.' I couldn't take it anymore and began to cry against all will.

Then with utter I-don't-know-what, my host mother put her arms around me and said, 'Oh see, you are still a little girl.' It was as if it was her aim all along to make me break. But I swallowed my tears and got over my initial shock and retaliated. First of all, I entirely disagree with her statement that I don't tell them stuff. Only an hour earlier I had been telling them all about the customs I had been lucky enough to participate in the night before, and on Sunday we'd been talking about Aboriginals – just to cite two examples. At this point Julia tried to intercept and say that she understands because she's the same. When asked about where she's been she likes to say, 'It was good,' and that's all. But she doesn't understand me at all. I like to talk about everything I've been doing, that's how it is with Mum at home. Here too I like to tell them when I have the chance, but it seems I don't do it enough.

The independent and getting involved aspect is only me carrying out what had been drummed into us at Rotary briefing weekends. But perhaps I have become too independent. They keep reminding me that I'm only a month older than Julia. I also like to be independent because I often think that if I rely on someone else it won't happen. Also the fact that all the other exchange students have counsellors and not me. I'm independent. I don't need one!

They also delivered the classic line, 'When you're older and have children of your own you'll understand our concerns about you returning at 10, 11 at night.' I understand now, but when they live so far from Warsaw and there is something of interest in Warsaw during the evening, there's no other way. And in any case, I don't return alone – I'm always with Daniel.

Well, in effect it's just a case of holding on another two weeks then I'll be in Austria for two weeks over Christmas, then back here for two weeks (but the weekend will be in the Mazurian Lakes), then home to Australia. Forty-five days.

I cried when I listened to the cassette and CDs of Australian Christmas carols my parents sent. They made me feel homesick.

Today I spent a few hours with Agnieszka. We met at 1 pm by the rotunda and first went to eat something at Pizza Hut and after that went to the Stare Miasto to a pub near the Barbican that does the best hot beer. It was nice to have some relaxed time to talk. Unfortunately my part of the conversation was clouded by what had happened this morning, but Agnieszka too had a problem she wanted to talk with me about.

Why do I feel so lethargic – physically and emotionally? I don't do anything physical, I eat a lot, I feel fat and my mind is tired from trying to rationalise things.

3-12-98

I've seen how both Alojzy and Julia treat their parents after returning from a year on exchange and I hope that I won't be like them – disrespectful, distant. I can't imagine this with my parents and me, as my parents are my best friends in the world. It was when my host mother made reference to them in her criticism of me that caused me to break. It seems Daniel's host mother is using similar tactics on him. He told me how she'd been threatening to write to his mother in Brazil and tell her about how he's so often coming home late, which is rather ridiculous after what Daniel has told me about his mother's liberal character. The funniest thing was that the same day a parcel arrived from his mum in Brazil. His host mother handed it to him and he thanked her. She said, 'Well, don't you want to open it and see what it is?' He felt it and said, 'No.' When she left the room he opened it, and sure enough inside he found half a dozen packets of condoms! Think of his host mum's reaction if he'd opened it in front of her!! In some ways I wish he had just to shock her but I would want to have been there to see her face. But then again, it implicates me, so I'm glad he didn't let her see it. I got rather embarrassed this morning when Daniel told me on the train that he got an email from his mum saying, 'I hope you and Jennifer have fun with the gift I sent.'

Well, it's the coldest November in 100 years in Poland. Even in Antarctica it's only -5°C, but here in Poland it's -20°C. It's so cold, but the whacky thing is the sun still shines and the sky is clear. So deceptive when you're looking through a window from the inside.

4-12-98

Today Daniel and I celebrated our three-month anniversary. But it feels like six. In fact it feels like we've known each other for years. We celebrated rather appropriately with some free drinks at the top of Warsaw's most prestigious hotel – the Marriot. So how did we manage to obtain free drinks in such a prestigious place I hear you ask? Well, as they say, it's who you know, not what you know. The son of a cool Rotarian works at the bar there and when his boss disappeared he slipped us a few free drinks. We felt quite posh sipping mixed drinks from long glasses amid fancy décor, listening to the jazz band playing and looking out on Warsaw 40 floors below, looking pretty with all its flashing Christmas lights. It wasn't just Daniel and me, Chloe and Cindy came too. We four get on really well, do heaps of stuff together, and I'm going to miss them. We had no particular reason for going up there tonight, other than the fact that it was one thing on my list of 'things-I-must-do-before-I-leave'. It wasn't until we were coming home on the train that we realised it was our three-month anniversary and thought, *well what a lovely evening we've had*. I knew it was for some purpose.

My first class now know that I'm leaving soon. They said, 'But you'll be coming back won't you? Who's going to teach us?' It made my heart heavy. I've become attached to my little students. It will be so sad to leave them. Mariusz too said it's a real shame I have to go. 'You just get to the stage where you can speak Polish really well and you have to leave,' he said.

It's strange but I'm more nervous when speaking Polish now than I was in the beginning. Now people expect me to be able to speak well so I'm more self-conscious, but when I arrived and couldn't speak Polish I had no qualms about trying, and made numerous amusing mistakes. Agata and I were reminiscing about this yesterday – my first day in Poland when I said '*Jestem gorąca*' (I'm hot, as in horny), instead of '*Jest mi gorąco*' (it's hot)!

Recently I listen a lot and understand everything but speak little, because the people I associate with at this time in my exchange are exchange students, my classes, Mariusz, Julia and Alojzy with whom I speak English. The times I speak Polish are only in Polish class, with my host parents and with friends from Lelewel or Promni. I listen to a lot – TV, radio, host parents, lecturer at Poly, Polish teacher and in the streets.

I could probably get to Polish class blind-folded now. After going to the same place twice a week for a semester prior to the summer holidays and this semester, it's pretty much second nature. Yet, even though I've taken that rickety lift up to the fourth floor of the building so many times, it was only the other day I noticed a sticker on the inside written in English. Before I tell you what was written there I first want to say that if you said the Marriot lift was the Mercedes of lifts you'd have to say the uni lift is the Polish Maluch Fiat of lifts. Rather pre-historic. The sticker read: 'Don't worry, 84% of Polish lifts are safe.'

5-12-98

I saw my first ever snowflake close up today. It's the first time I've examined one close up and seen its amazing form. I always thought that the snowflake shapes people drew and made from paper were just romanticised versions of a drop of snow. Now I know there's some science in it.

Daniel came by at one-ish and we went sledding in the park. It was heaps of fun. We used his host family's sled. The park at the end of the street is great as it has slopes leading down to the frozen lake. There were many kids there with their fathers, taking advantage of the newly fallen snow. And there was us two, neither kids nor fathers, just foreigners to the sledding experience.

7-12-98

It's all on to get everything organised for Christmas before I go to Austria. I'm just about meeting someone different every day – all my Warsaw friends, to give them their Christmas presents. At the same time I'm doing gift shopping for Australia because I want to buy Polish things and may not have the chance when I come back from Austria.

I'm on my host mother's good side today as I returned for *obiad* and sat and listened to her for 1½ hours. No seriously, we had a good conversation today about all sorts of social and psychological things. I understood everything and gave my opinion on various topics.

It's already 12.40 am but I must write otherwise I'll get too far behind.

Yesterday we had a family trip. We went to the ruins of Warsaw's first castle – about 30 kilometres out of Warsaw. It used to be right on the bank of the Vistula but the river changed course. Next we went to the house in Warka, now a museum, where Kazimierz Pułaski, a national hero of both Poland and America, was born.

In the evening I wrote Christmas cards. My hand was sore after writing 30-something times:

Wesołych Świąt Bożego Narodzenia i szczęśliwego Nowego Roku
[Merry Christmas and a Happy New Year]

My parents sent me 60 Australian Christmas cards which aren't going to be enough.

This morning I spent an hour at Lelewel. It was the hour with their homeroom teacher and they were doing secret Santa, or as they call it here *Swieta Mikołajki*. I was very surprised when I received a present – a *bocian* [stork] stuffed toy. They are very important birds in Poland. I'd just been reading in my book, *Poland*, about the anti-Nazi rebellion group who called themselves the stork commandos. I gave out all my cards and felt really bad because I forgot one person. I always get two girls mixed up and must have thought I'd already done hers when I hadn't.

Now that I have only forty days left, and only nineteen of those in Poland, my family have suddenly become interested in taking me places and showing me things. Tomorrow morning my host father is taking the morning off work to take me to Wilanów. Although I've been there many times, I've never been inside the castle itself.

This evening I made rum balls, some of which are going to be a present for Tym's family who I'm visiting tomorrow. Just as I had sticky chocolate mixture all over my hands Daniel came. He'd forgotten his keys. He didn't stay for long though because when he called home Antoni had already arrived. It was long enough for a kiss behind my mother's back. Tomorrow he's going to come with us.

Oh dear, I'm getting so fat. I'm eating more because of the cold and not getting any exercise. I'm going to return to Australia white-skinned and fat right in the middle of the summer holidays – swimsuit weather.

8-12-98

I had the best kiss ever today. I really love him. I had to convince him of this today as he still isn't sure that I'm not just stringing him along. I said that for a while I had doubts. I love him for who he is even though some of the things he does annoy me now and then. The more time goes on the deeper I love him and the more comfortable I feel with him, and that inner voice trying to prevent me getting too involved for the sake of my future becomes less and less audible.

Today my host father took Daniel and me to Wilanów. To our bad luck we discovered that on Tuesdays it's closed. Instead we looked at a Poster exhibition. Josef dropped us off afterwards near my *politechnika* building. I still had an hour till my lesson so I said to Daniel, 'Let's go for some tea in the café downstairs.' We got so involved in our conversation that we lost track of time and the next time I glanced at my watch it was already 10 minutes into my lesson so I decided I wasn't going to go.

Later I made my way to Łomianki. In the dark and with everything covered in snow it was difficult to recognise where to get off. The last time I visited Tym's family was in summer and I was wearing shorts and a T-shirt. They liked the rum balls I made and they gave me a present too. I was a good girl and didn't open it. I'll save it and take it to Austria for Christmas

Day. I'm not in love with Tym anymore – he's just a good mate with whom to have a few laughs and good conversations.

Tonight I had to lie to my host father about my lesson today. It's the first time I've played truant and later lied about it.

The snow gets deeper and deeper every day. About 25 centimetres now. There were even people skiing along our street yesterday. 100 people died in one week from the cold in Poland. And still my host father says winter hasn't started yet – winter doesn't start till around 21st December.

'Character is the sum of all we do before the age of twenty.'

A line I read in my book today. An interesting one. I already know that this year has had a big influence on my character. Just the other day I was thinking about how timely it is that I'm doing such an exchange now. Not just in terms of the stage I'm at in my life, where things are changing and I'm making the transition from child to adult, but also in terms of the stage Poland is at right now – making the transition from a poor communist country to a democratic one with enormous economic potential. It makes for a very exciting time.

17-12-98

What a busy week this last week has been. I've been rushing from one side of Warsaw to the other delivering presents to everyone I know before departing. The weather hasn't made it any easier either. Although it's a more comfortable temperature, all the sparkling white snow has turned to slippery slush which demands head down and careful treading at all times when going on foot. And of course, rather than falling snowflakes, it's raindrops. Traffic jams are the order of the day. But never mind, I managed to achieve just about all I set out to do.

Any free moment I found during the following few days I was making mince pies. Every night I didn't get to bed until midnight or after due to one type of preparation or another that needed to be made for Christmas.

Sunday I was invited for *obiad* with Agnieszka and her family. I arrived promptly at 2 pm. Unfortunately her parents had had to leave for Lublin where an uncle of theirs was sick, but she had prepared some delicious food for us, so we ate and chatted and exchanged presents. We ate bean soup followed by some Lithuanian dumplings made of potatoes and meat, and afterwards some cake that Agnieszka had made. They gave me a lovely hardback picture book about Poland. I didn't let them open their presents though. They have to save them for Christmas.

That evening I went for supper with Daniel and his host family. Daniel made some Brazilian cheese bread and I delivered my presents to his host family. In the hall on my way in, it was fortunate that I came upon Antoni, while Daniel was still busy in the kitchen. I gave him my present for Daniel and asked him to hide it and only bring it out for Christmas. Last night Daniel gave me a present which I am not allowed to open till Christmas either. He said he'd wanted to give it secretly to Mr Nowak but hadn't had the opportunity. I said 'I'm sorry I haven't got you anything!' Little does he know.

Finally I got to the Muzeum Etnograficzne where there was a meeting organised by the Centre Polonicum where I have Polish lessons. The purpose was to tell us about Polish Christmas traditions. There were many people there from many different countries, all eager to learn. First they explained them and showed us various things, and after that we had the opportunity to make Christmas decorations, eat Christmas food and sing carols. It was great, I loved it. The other exchange students were there too, other than Brooke who had to work. I saw my two teachers – the first one I had, such a sweet old lady, was delighted to see me and interested to know when I was going back and so on. She asked me straight out, 'Do you have a boyfriend here?' 'Well, yes,' I answered, 'but he's not Polish, he's Brazilian.' 'Oh that doesn't matter,' she said. 'You just need to have some love and fun in your life.' She is such a sweet dear.

I finished making my straw star and straw angel then I went downstairs to join the exchange students for a beer in the pub.

Wednesday was a big day. Polish exam in the morning, my last English lessons with my children in the afternoon and the Rotary Christmas party in the evening. I think I did OK in the exam. I'll get the results and a certificate before I return to Australia. The theme of my last lesson with my English students was Christmas in Australia. We sang Australian Christmas carols and made some decorations for the Christmas tree. I got them to cut out the shape of a gum leaf from green cardboard, tie on a red ribbon then dab some eucalyptus oil on it. While they were doing this they could taste it by sucking on a eucalyptus sweet, so it was all about the five senses which they learned to say in English.

Mariusz very generously drove me all the way to Aleksandrów (an hour out of Warsaw) where the Rotary Christmas party was being held. It was important for me to be at my last lessons with my classes and to be at the Rotary *Wigilia* [Christmas], and without Mariusz volunteering to drive me, one of them would have to have been forfeited because there would have been no other way to get there. Unexpected presents came from all angles that evening.

I returned with Daniel's host parents and spent about 1½ hours at their place. It gave Daniel and I a proper chance to say goodbye for the next two weeks, and wish each other a Merry

Christmas. I played my Australian carols CD which sounded great in their cavernous house – just like a church. It is around now that the Nine Lessons and Carols will be taking place at my church at home. It's not until now that I realise how important for me this event is. It's the first year in many that I am missing it. As I said to Daniel last night, choir was just something I did every Sunday morning and Tuesday night – enjoyed it and didn't think much of it, but this year being away from it has brought me to realise that it was an important part of my life. Not because I have a good voice, but simply for the enjoyment of singing with a group of people to the one who has given me such a glorious life of wonderful experiences.

Austria

17-12-98 continued

Here I am somewhere in the south of Poland leaning against a wall in a mechanic's workshop. It's 8 pm. We should be halfway through the Czech Republic by now, but we've had a breakdown. Our destination (that is Mr Nowak and me) is Vienna for tonight, but at this rate it looks like we'll be getting there in the dark hours of the morning. Tomorrow is my day in Vienna – free to explore as I choose. We're staying with friends of Mr Nowak. Either tomorrow evening or the following morning we'll drive to Klagenfurt, to Mr Nowak's house and family where I'll be spending Christmas and New Year.

Well it's now 9.30 pm and it's bloody cold and I'm hungry...
...but life's good!

Later...
How did we get out of our difficult situation in southern Poland, I hear you ask? Well...

After three hours at the mechanic's, who didn't tell us much, we decided to risk it and keep driving to Vienna. The problem was an oil leak, so we bought a lot of oil and just kept refilling every 100 kilometres. We finally arrived in Vienna at 4.30 am. Mr Nowak's friends, with whom I was to stay, live in the penthouse of an inner-city apartment. Rather flash, but they're lovely people. They both work and both speak English well.

They have two little girls. They have spent some time living in Poland too. The first thing they did after the greetings was give me a house key, tell me that they would be gone in the morning but to get what I like out of the fridge for breakfast. They said, 'a map of the city is on the table, our cleaner will be here in the morning, and come back for a meal between 3 pm and 4 pm.' With that I went to bed. I woke up about 10 am and while I showered the cleaner made me breakfast. The POLISH cleaner. Sure enough, their cleaner is a Polish lady, so we had quite a chat in Polish – what I'm doing in Vienna, what she's doing in Vienna and so on.

By 11 am I was out of the house and on my way to explore Vienna. I didn't have much time but I got a taste of this city where there are 'grand façades hiding the hypocrisy within'. It reminded me of Stockholm in feel – i.e. style of buildings, cleanness, weather and classiness, but also of Prague and Budapest in format, being based around a river.

I took a walk around the Ringstrasse. First stop was the *Rathaus* or town hall. A grand building. In front of it was the *Christkindl* market. Each city in Austria had one of these. Here you can buy all sorts of Christmas-related things, from decorations to cakes to presents. I saw all these people eating large round bready things and drinking hot fruity wine stuff and decided; *I'll have what they're having.* So I found my way to where such things were being sold and got some. I sat eating and drinking on a park bench looking towards the Rathaus. When I'd finished I had a souvenir cup with which to remember the experience, and for the rest of the day it became my companion to which I spoke about what I saw (either in English or Polish).

Next stop was the art gallery where I spent an hour or so looking at the fine collection of European paintings.

I walked up the classiest shopping street with its wonderful shop window displays, fascinating buildings and lovely Christmas decorations. Here I picked up some information about concerts in the evening. I came to St. Stephen's Square and St. Stephen's Cathedral – a gothic one, which I looked inside. I walked back along the Danube and arrived at home about 3.30 pm.

The mother and elder daughter were at home, and at about 5 pm, Hanz arrived with the younger daughter, and we all sat down and ate a meal together. It was meat, potatoes and salad. I had said earlier that I was interested in going to a concert and showed them the brochures I had collected. They called for me and organised the ticket. So after dinner I went to a Mozart concert. My concert was in a small room whose walls were decorated with baroque-style paintings. The string quartet played various works of Mozart including *Eine kleine Nachtmuzik*. It was very pleasant, and now I can say I've attended a Mozart concert in Vienna. I was quite willing to pay for it as on Wednesday I had received my final pay for teaching, and Mariusz gave me a bonus as he was so pleased with my work. So I had some money to spend on myself. But Hanz wouldn't let me.

20-12-98

Here I am back in Maria Rain with the Nowaks. It feels as if I've come home. I love this family. Carly isn't here, she's visiting her grandmother in Germany, and ever since I've arrived they've been unloading all their complaints about Carly onto me, and explaining to me all the problems they've been having with her. It seems to me that America sends out as exchange students those who need some experience of the world because they are too narrow-minded. Australia sends out as exchange students those who will be good ambassadors of Australia and later will be able to share with other Australians their experience of another country. Meanwhile, if you go on exchange from Poland you're either the daughter or son of a Rotarian, or you're looking to finish your schooling in a country where the education system is not as difficult as in Poland. Anyway, that's enough of that.

It was a three-hour drive from Vienna to Maria Rain. Mr Nowak was so glad to be home. I too thought; *Ahhh, now I can relax a bit and have time to make Christmas decorations, make cakes, write my leaving speech, read and whatever.* But no, I'm non-stop on the go again.

Yesterday evening, Oskar and I went to Klagenfurt to drink some *gluhwein* – hot Austrian wine, and after that to an underground pub for beer. We had some good conversations. He's finished his schooling here in Austria now and will complete his final two years in Poland. After that he may do an exchange to Australia through the Warsaw Rotary club. It would be funny if we ended up hosting him.

Anyway, we returned by bus and walked the 7 kilometres uphill home. It was a beautiful starry night, a light covering of snow lay on the ground and majestic fir trees loomed around. The air was cool and fresh.

Today we had more fresh air. All of us, after breakfast, went by car a little way into the mountains and we walked along a ridge looking at the wonderful view of mountains all around. I climbed up a ladder attached to a tree which lead to a platform at the top from which there was a great view. It was very high and without a safety rope. My heart was beating fast as I ascended and descended, but it was worth it.

23-12-98

I'm visiting Carly's high school today. We're in German class right now. I don't understand anything of course but I'm making it look like I'm doing some work by writing in my diary. It's a nice school; clean, modern facilities and small class sizes. Being the last day of school before the Christmas break, it's not so serious. The first lesson we spent watching a video.

It's only a half day (four lessons) and then we're going back to the internet café that we were at yesterday. Yes, we discovered Klagenfurt's two computers in the corner of a café above the bank which qualifies it to be called the Internet café. Anyway, I had 6 new messages, all written with the assumption that they would be read when I returned to Warsaw. I wrote a quick one to Mum and Dad.

It's not just life in Poland and Europe and friends here and the exchange experience that I'm going to miss when I go home, but also writing to my parents. We've built up quite a writing relationship which we never had, well, never needed before. I have really enjoyed emailing them (usually once or twice a week) and telling them everything I've been doing, and reading their replies of what they're up to, and their jokes, making me laugh out loud on many occasions. It's a strange thing but when you have such a relationship with someone your mind's image of them can be whatever you please, and I guess, most often than not, it's not affected by the passage of time. The image in my mind when I set out to write to my parents is of a youthful, active, smiling couple, overflowing with love and humour, liberal in their out-look and more like friends than parents. Most of these qualities I'm sure are still true, but I got a little shock when they called on the morning before I left Warsaw, at how old they sounded. I forgot all the things I wanted to tell them. It's so much more difficult to speak with them than write to them. It took me a few minutes to get used to their accent and they said I sounded strange too. I'm sure it will all be different when we're back together again. (I hope so.)

I believe that when you set out on a journey with the knowledge of your return date, your mind subconsciously prepares you for that. Over the last month or two I've been on a bit of an emotional rollercoaster; feeling sad that I'm leaving soon, but happy to be returning home. Sad at leaving behind all that has become part of my life in Poland and Europe, then happy that soon I'll be with my family and friends and hot weather. But now, like Keats in 'To Autumn', I'm coming to an acceptance of the closing of a chapter in my life. The best chapter of my life so far.

'And gathering swallows twitter in the skies.'

I've been thinking back over my amazing year as I gather together all my thoughts for my final speech at Rotary. I've been writing a little each day and Mr and Mrs Nowak have been helping me.

Yesterday Carly, Mrs Nowak and I went shopping. I bought a dress to wear for Christmas because I left my good outfit in Vienna. Beata [Mrs Nowak] was great to go clothes shopping with. I admire her a lot. She's spent the last 20 years being a housewife – raising her children in a country whose language she didn't know when she arrived and had no time for lessons. She'll be very happy to move to Warsaw I think. They're not the only family I know who are moving back to Poland. Things in Poland are improving all the time – lifestyle, career opportunities, education etc. Those who previously fled from a poor, socialist country are now returning to their homeland.

We've bought our really truly Christmas tree! It was quite an experience for me. We got it from a local garden centre and carried it home on the top of the Jeep. Agnieszka told me that when she was a baby, which was during the revolutionary times in Warsaw when Russian tanks were on the streets, and people had to be in their homes by 10 pm, her father got a Christmas tree in Ursynów [South Warsaw]. He carried it physically all the way by himself to their apartment in Żoliborz [North Warsaw] so that his young family would have a tree for Christmas.

Last night Carly and I made some decorations, but as tradition goes, they won't be put on the tree until the evening of the 24th. I taught Carly how to make some Polish decorations from straw and Carly taught me how to make some German decorations from paper. She has recently returned from visiting her grandmother in Germany and that's where she learned it. She came back Monday night. During the day I made 60 mince pies.

The preparations for *Wigilia* are almost done so perhaps we'll be able to go skating or skiing tomorrow. I hope so – I can't wait.

25-12-98

MERRY CHRISTMAS
WESOŁYCH ŚWIĄT
FROHE WEIHNACHTEN

My European Christmas was a fantastic experience. I've just been relating it to my parents who called this morning. It's the evening of the 25th there and they spent the day on the beach. Mine was a white Christmas celebrated on the 24th as is the Polish custom.

We began by going ice-skating on a nearby frozen lake. There was Carly, Oskar and me, and we spent 2 hours there. It was great to have the freedom of an open-air lake, few people and comfortable skates (borrowed from Elena, Oskar's sister who is on exchange in America). I fell three times – well, four if you count the time Oskar caused me to fall. We were pretending to be figure skaters and I was so pleased I could skate backwards and in a circle.

When we got home we all got washed and dressed up into our nice outfits. I put on my new dress and after being used to layers and jumpers was a little cold in short sleeves, but soon enough we had a log fire going in the living room.

The next task was to decorate the tree. (The really truly tree.) We hung it with the German stars we'd made, and the walnut shell animals we'd made. There were also balls, bows, chocolates, beads, cinnamon sticks and lots more. It looked really pretty and was placed so it would be seen from the lounge room as well as the dining room.

Once it was dark (about 4.30 pm) we began *Wigilia* – the festive supper. First we broke the communion bread together – *opłatek*. Each person takes a piece then goes around sharing it with everyone else and wishing them a merry Christmas. I also shared the one Felix from the Polish Association had sent me from Australia and the one Agnieszka had given me in Warsaw.

We didn't try and stick to the traditional 12 courses. Five was enough. We began with *śledź* (herring): one in curry sauce and one with cream and onion, the latter being the Polish traditional style. With it was bread and vegetable salad. Second was *barszcz* (beetroot soup) with *uszka* (small dumplings with mushrooms inside). Third was carp with vegetable salad and potato salad. Here we had a break and opened our presents. The rustling of paper lasted about 10 minutes then everything was suddenly quiet. It was nice not to be the youngest and to have my presents delivered to me, and to be able to watch the joy of a young child opening presents.

We returned to the table to finish the meal – fruit salad then tea and cakes. There was the traditional *makowiec* (poppy seed cake) and also – my influence – mince pies.

Adjourning to the lounge room where the fire burned, we sang carols – Polish, Australian, American. We sang 'Silent Night' in three languages – a verse in Polish, a verse in German and a verse in English. That was really nice. It's so fascinating living with a family where there are three languages between us. It makes games rather fun. We played Uno, and when announcing the colours we had to repeat it in the two languages we know so that everyone would understand.

We went to the midnight Mass in Klagenfurt. As we entered the bells were chiming. Mum and Dad said they also heard the bells from the church in Klagenfurt – on a radio program presented by Karl Haas entitled *Bells of Europe* or something like that! Klagenfurt is a pretty baroque church and we heard the choir sing 'Silent Night' in its original language.

We came home, all rather cold, and drank hot *gluhwein* in front of the fire before going to bed. And that was my Christmas with the Nowaks in Klagenfurt, Austria!

26-12-98

It's a non-stop sit-com living in this family. There's always jokes and laughter and mucking around. I feel closer to this family than either of my two host families. I'm beginning to think of them as my third host family. It just occurred to me that I've experienced living first as an only child, second with a sister, and now with brothers. I prefer brothers.

Yesterday, after a late breakfast and phone call from Grandma and Grandpa, we went ice-skating again. There were more people this time, but the sun was shining and the whole family went. We stayed three hours and by the end I was feeling quite confident. There were all ages on the ice – parents pulling toddlers on sleds, elderly pairs slowly gliding around, energetic young men and women playing ice-hockey, toddlers in all-in-ones slipping and sliding etc. After all that fresh air and exercise, a good meal, some garlic and horseradish on bread (as I felt a cold coming on) and a seat in front of the fire, I was sooooo sleepy but comfortable sleepy. You'll never guess what film was on TV in the evening. *Babe*, the Australian movie about a pig. We all sat down to watch it and they loved it. Twelve-year-old Jackub particularly liked the mice with their occasional comic appearances as his nickname is 'mouse'. Beata said, 'Isn't that a coincidence that in the morning the bells of the Klagenfurt church are heard in Australia over the radio, and in the evening we watch an Australian movie on the TV?'

Tomorrow we're going skiing. I tried on Elena's skiing pants and was given Jackub's sweater and now have my skiing outfit which looks quite stylish. I'm hoping hard that my cold won't get any worse.

19 days to go.

28-12-98

There are advantages to being short. I was able to borrow Beata's skis and hence have my first experience of skiing in the Austrian Alps. Carly, on the other hand, who is tall and has big feet, was unable to ski. In this part of Austria there is no possibility to hire skis as everyone has their own. I'm sure, however, if she'd asked, or rather, made it clear that she was interested, the Nowaks would have somehow found a pair to fit. The problem is she lacks initiative. Later, when we were alone in our bedroom,

I had a chat to her and tried to encourage her to take more initiative. Being an exchange student is a totally different way of living. You must put aside certain manners you'd been brought up to follow, such as waiting to be invited rather than inviting yourself. If the exchange student is not a little selfish in terms of inviting themself to places and asking to be taken places, then not much will happen in the life of the exchange student. It's not up to the natives to fit this variable into their norm but rather that the exchange student as a variable fits into the norm.

Anyway, I thoroughly enjoyed my skiing experience. The last and only time I've skied was at the age of about eight in the Snowy Mountains, NSW, on a Brownie-organised camp for about 4 days. I was so excited that I was going skiing that I didn't think about whether I was able to or not. I put on the skis and then it occurred to me: *Oh. What do I do now?* Mr and Mrs Nowak acted as my instructors, refreshing my memory of what I had been taught as an eight-year-old. After a few exercises at the bottom of the hill I was ready to hit the baby lift. It goes halfway up the mountain and is free. I managed a few goes of that before it was time for us to leave and I only fell once. I do hope I get the chance to go back.

Tomorrow Jackub goes into hospital to have his tonsils out. Carly and I have decided to go to Salzburg for the day. We only decided it an hour ago. Alternatively we could have gone to the heated pool in Klagenfurt which I would love to, but Carly is embarrassed to wear a swimsuit in public. The other thing I would have loved to do was go skiing again but, of course, Carly doesn't have any skis. We could go ice-skating again – something we'd both like to do, but we don't have transport. So going to Salzburg is something that is both possible and something we'd both like to do.

17 days to go.

29-12-98

I've never heard so many Australian accents in one day. Salzburg seems a popular place for Australian tourists at this time of year. It's easy to see why – it's a gorgeous town. I love that place and we had a great day there.

Our planning, as last minute as it was, turned out to be very good. We made the best use of the daylight – starting out on the 7.27 am train and riding it through breathtaking Austrian landscape in its morning freshness. For the train ride itself, it was worth it. We saw frozen waterfalls, villages nestling in deep valleys and towering snow-covered craggy mountains.

We arrived at 10.45 am and made our way on foot straight to Mozartplaz. The great thing about Salzburg is it has a compact centre. Mozartplaz of course centres around a monument of its namesake who was born in a street not far from there. Here also is the *Glockenspiel*, Archbishop's residence, gallery and cathedral.

The summit, or climax, of the day was to reach the fortress on the hill and take in the sunlit view of the city and its beautiful roofline and icy green river running through the middle. A colour that reminded me immediately of the rivers in New Zealand.

I found here, in the souvenir shop, the T-shirt I had to have. White, with this on the front:

From here we worked our way back, along Gold Street, a narrow boutique-lined and handsomely decorated street, into the main shopping street where we sampled apple strudel and cappuccino in a cosy café, past Mozart's birthplace, back over the river to St. Sebastian Church and the graveyard of well-known Renaissance masters, past the house of Doppler (i.e. Doppler effect) and through the gardens where scenes from *The Sound of Music* had been filmed.

We arrived back at the station and were getting on the train just as it became dark.

It's funny how whenever I hear an Aussie accent it's, *wow! That person is from Australia.* In 16 days I'm going to be amid people who all speak with an Australian accent. It's going to be wow! Wow!! Wow!!!

31-12-98

It's New Year's Eve but it doesn't feel like the end of the year – the 14th will be the end of the year for me.

I miss Daniel. I guess he'll be in Karwica now. I'm being haunted by the stupid Cher computerised song that goes:

'Do you believe in life after love
I hear something inside me say
I really don't think you're strong enough.'
[Cher, 'Believe']

Perhaps it's trying to tell me something. I hear it everywhere I go.

Yesterday Oskar and I went to the indoor sports complex and went swimming for 2 hours. There were various pools of different sizes and a water slide that went out of the building, spun around a few times and came back inside to deliver you into the pool. It's a really cool place. It was weird to be looking out through large windows on a snow-covered streetscape and yet be wearing swimmers in a warm pool. Carly didn't come with us as she's embarrassed about wearing a swimsuit in public. I don't have a great figure either, plus I had to borrow swimmers of the style I would never buy for myself (high cut), but I love swimming and it's not like I know anybody there.

1-1-99

All this fresh air and exercise seems to be making my eyes bluer and my lips redder. I spent the evening of the first day of the year skiing by the light of the full moon and a few floodlights. Quite a rush.

I saw in the New Year with Carly, Oskar and a group of his friends from school in the city. We were at a house near the centre for a while drinking and dancing, then at 11.40 pm we joined the crowds in the square for the count down. I only drank two glasses of champagne and a vodka and orange juice, but the way I was feeling suggested that whoever made it put in mostly vodka and not much orange juice. I was swaying a little more than everyone else but I was happy.

Three days ago I said to Carly, 'Before I go I hope to go skiing again, ice-skating again and swimming.' Today I went skiing, yesterday ice-skating and the day before that swimming. So, I couldn't ask for anything more.

3-1-99

On the road again. Mist is hanging heavily in the air, and in my head is hanging heavily the real weight of the end approaching.

Just 11 days more.

Yesterday I spent the whole day writing my farewell speech for Rotary and typing it up on the Nowak's computer. Meanwhile, the Nowaks were packing half the house for the first stage of their move to Warsaw. Olek and Oskar are the first to move, and Olek will return for his wife and Jackub in February.

I will miss this family – I had a great time with them and felt the most at home there. Through helping me with my speech they know everything I've done during the year. Just a few minutes ago we counted up how many European capitals I've been to this year. The answer is nine: Warsaw, London, Dublin, Paris, Madrid, Prague, Budapest, Stockholm and Vienna.

We were listening to Olek's driving tape a little while ago (Polish drinking songs) and I began to sing along – so that shows that I've travelled with him more than once. In fact, four times between Warsaw and Klagenfurt – a total of 48 hours.

Podkowa Leśna

I returned to Warsaw to discover that my host grandfather had died of cancer on New Year's Eve. Three days previous to that, a cousin of my host father died. Both funerals are this week so it's a difficult and sad time in my host family at the moment. Here's that song again – playing now on the radio:

'Goodbye my friend
It's not the end.'
[The Spice Girls, 'Goodbye']

I stayed home today and made a start in sorting out my stuff into what to take home, what to leave behind and what to chuck out. I made a lot of phone calls this evening mainly to find out who can come to Karwica on the weekend. The last one was to Tym who answered my Polish with English which made me tongue-tied, because I had just had several conversations in Polish, was used to speaking Polish and didn't want to revert to English. It's a strange thing but I feel more confident speaking Polish on the phone than English. During this year my confidence has built as has my ability in Polish. The two are tied together. When I start speaking English I revert to my shy self. I never used to call somebody at home without first planning what I was going to say. Here I've already dialled the number before I think what to say, and that's in my second language. I understand just about everything now. These last two weeks have been good for that. It's fun to be able to complete someone's sentence for them when they get stuck.

Also, thanks to the phone calls I made tonight, my next few days are organised. I also spoke to Agnieszka tonight who told me that her uncle died over Christmas. All these people dying. But that's life I guess.

5-1-99

I'd go home tomorrow if I could. All these goodbyes (and there'll be plenty more to come) are getting me down. Today I saw my first host family for the last time. They gave me my Christmas present (a silver tiger) and a present each for my parents. Alojzy left about an hour before I did to go to the internet café and look up his High School Certificate results. When I got home there was a phone call and explanation needed of what it all meant. It's such a stupid, complicated system. In short he didn't do very well, but considering English isn't his first language it was pretty good.

Daniel called from Mazury this evening where he's been since the 28th and will stay for the weekend when I and everyone I've invited will join him for my farewell party weekend. My Christmas and New Year were much more exciting than his.

Warsaw is a different place compared to when I left. No snow, plus temperatures, and a little bit of sunshine.

7-1-99

More goodbyes today – to those dead and alive. It was the funeral of my host grandfather. Many people, many flowers, much sadness. As I sat in the church staring at the coffin and listening to the soloist sing the 'Ave Maria' to a tune I know well, my sadness went in two directions. Firstly I felt a deep sympathy for my host family – my host mother, an only child like me, just lost her father. Julia now has only one grandmother left, and I have all four grandparents still. Secondly, the whole event seemed to symbolise the death of my year in Poland – the end of a glorious chapter. I can rejoice in the glories that were and the achievements I made, but I'm sorrowful that it's ending.

As we stood in the cemetery, in exactly the same place we stood two months ago for All Souls Day, I recognised the uncanny juxtaposition of it all. He was with us then, but in life, and no-one had any idea that within two months we'd all be back in the same place to bid farewell to one who stood among us. The heavens, like then, now cried too.

I also looked on the event from another angle – that it was yet another cultural experience. A point that was mentioned to me later, when we had returned home, by none other than the widow herself. She's a very wise and kind lady. She said to me, 'Now you've experienced both the sad aspects as well as the joyful aspects of Polish life.'

I went to Promni for the last time tonight. It was a nice one to end on. We sang through a variety of songs and the dancing was a little livelier than usual. I could see how their week in the mountains together over New Year had bonded the group and its new members. I said a quiet goodbye to those I was fond of, and to the Director who gave me the Promni CD-ROM as a gift.

Yesterday I did a lot of walking around the centre of Warsaw shopping for gifts to take home. Some success but more required. At 5 pm I met Gizela and Mariusz at the Palace of Culture and we went to the posh café on the Plac Trzech Krzyzy that I'd always walked past and wondered what it was like. We spent a lovely 1½ hours together chatting about the year and plans for the future. Gizela gave me a little book of Polish poetry with a beautiful message inside the front cover in Polish which when translated reads:

> 'Dear Jennifer
> To remember your stay in Poland.
> Thank you for your interest and enthusiasm.
> It was super to meet you and be friends with you.'

Mariusz gave me a book of aerial photographs of Poland inside which he had slotted an eye-watering reference with regards to my work as a counsellor on the camp and as a teacher of English. I'm so happy I met them. They are a wonderful pair. I love their enthusiasm for life and cultures, both their own and others.

After Rotary, everyone invited me to go out to a pub. I said, 'But my host mother asked me to get the earlier train as Daniel is not here to accompany me home.' Olek and Maksym, both Rotarians, said, 'Go out with your friends, you've only a week left in Poland.' So I went, and enjoyed it. There was Oskar and Tym in addition to the American girls. Alojzy was at the meeting but didn't come out with us afterwards. It was my last farewell to him also as he flies to France on Sunday to study there.

Tomorrow it's off to the Lakes (Karwica) for the weekend – a farewell party weekend. The guest list began with 14, now there are 7 going – three of whom are joining us a day late. It's a bad time of year really as everyone has exams. That's the reason why Tym, Alina, Pieter and Oskar aren't coming. Unfortunately Agnieszka is sick again which is why she isn't coming. I'm really disappointed about that because the same thing happened with Sopot. It's important she gets well though. Julia was the other one. She's not coming for a number of reasons – work and a special Mass that's being held in honour of her grandfather on Saturday. Nevertheless I'm sure we'll have fun anyway.

Karwica

8-1-99

'Look thy last on all things lovely every hour.'
[Walter de la Mare, 'Fare Well']

This quote, a favourite of my mum's, popped into my head as we were driving through the distinctive flat Polish landscape, and it came upon me a sudden little jump of excitement that in a week I'll see her again.

10-1-99

My farewell weekend in Karwica was nice but not particularly special. It would have been great if all the others I'd invited had been there but as I expected there was too much of an American presence when I wanted it to be Polish. Martyna was my only Polish friend there, but that was better than no Polish friends at all. There were the four American girls and of course Daniel and me.

The first evening was spoiled by Daniel who drank too much. Not something you do on the first night if you want to enjoy the rest. But I didn't let it ruin my weekend.

On Saturday we set off for our day trip. First stop was a church and monastery called Święta Lipka, another of Poland's places of religious pilgrimage. It was really cold and we had to stand and wait outside for about 15 minutes until the monks had finished their lunch before we could be let inside the church. It's a very beautiful building, particularly from the outside, but the most entertaining thing about our visit was the little priest who gave us a tour. He had no end of enthusiasm for this place and delightedly told us of its history as if he'd just discovered it himself. As he talked his arms flailed expressively and his eyes danced.

Next stop was somewhat different. We went swimming in a hotel in Mikołajki. It's a fantastic place, better than the one in Klagenfurt. It has several different types of pools and water-slides, all on different levels with bridges and steps – cool design. We spent an hour and a half there trying out everything from hot tubs to tunnel waterslides and whirlpools.

By the time we got home – about 6 pm, everyone was so hungry. We ate delicious *zurek* which I'd requested, *bigos* which I'd requested, and *pączek* which I'd requested. Prepared by Maksym whose life hobby is cooking. He has his own show on national TV.

In the evening and on into the night we had a bonfire outside. We all dressed up warm, brushed the snow off the benches and sat around the fire singing songs and eating steak and chicken and sausages that were being cooked on the BBQ. It was lots of fun. I had my state flag draped around me and gave everyone a taste of vegemite.

There was beer, but Wicek our counsellor, who is much stricter than the other guys, was keeping an eye on us. We were given a half-cup each as a symbolic gesture, but after that we were just helping ourselves anyway.

Later we moved inside for champagne and cakes. Wicek poured the champagne filling the cups halfway and leaving the bottle with still a third in it. Then Maksym came along and took the bottle and filled the cups finishing off the bottle. It was quite amusing. Maksym is a Communist but he's a very nice man, very generous, kind and fun-loving.

They made a toast to me – a safe return to Australia and all the best with my studies in architecture. I too said a few words thanking them for the weekend, saying that this year had been the best experience in my life and that for sure I'll come back one day.

Daniel and I drank the remains of my vodka bottle – still the same one I got for my birthday from Tym. An appropriate occasion to finish it.

Today, Sunday, we went ice-fishing on the lake. Something new for me and I took lots of pictures. First Maksym dug a hole in the ice, then threw down some food and finally set the rods in position. Then you just have to wait for a bite. Or if you are Kasimierz, wait for the computer to beep its alarm! Yes that's right, Kasimierz has this special computer that takes readings from a small radar stuck in the hole, and on the screen you can watch the fish swimming by. He had it set up away from us, in the middle of the huge lake that was completely frozen with 30 centimetres of ice, and lightly covered in snow. It was an amazing view, just this whiteness stretching on forever. It was also very, very cold. We kept hearing the ice spasming and got quite scared, but they assured us that's normal and there's no danger. I didn't personally catch any fish, but I tried and it was good to do it once for the experience.

Just three days left. I'm no longer concerned about trying to pack in a program of places I still haven't been and things I still haven't done. I'm not worried about that because I'm too excited that I'm going home.

14-1-99

Well, what an emotional 3 days it has been. Monday and Tuesday I spent shopping for presents for my family and friends in Oz. Daniel accompanied me and helped me out, and it was nice to spend the time with him. On Monday we took a break to drink coffee in the African coffee house in the Old Town. It's a tiny place (only three tables) but a lovely cosy atmosphere and great coffee. Only three tables and yet, at one of the other two sat two girls who were speaking with an Australian accent. A strange feeling came over me – it was my last days in Poland and I didn't want to hear Australian English, I wanted to hear Polish. Anyway, our café interlude was one of many special moments between Daniel and I. One that will become part of the series of beautiful memories of him.

On Tuesday, the other exchange students took me out to lunch. It was Cindy's idea, and a lovely one, but it was a case of 'We're inviting you, but you choose the place, the day, the time and we'll be there'. I guess that was better though because I enjoy things better when I've organised them myself. Daniel and I were talking about this and he said that on this point I'm rather egotistical. I can't leave organisation up to someone else because I'm afraid it won't turn out. I'm a little tired of organising everything myself though. I'd like to have things organised for me for a change.

We went to a restaurant in the Old Town. Not too expensive, with traditional Polish food. In addition to the exchange students was Oskar and afterwards we all went back to his family's new apartment for a few hours. It is in a very similar style to their house in Austria – antique furniture and white walls.

That evening I had a farewell supper with my host family. It was a lovely occasion.

Wednesday was the worst day ever. Everything that could possibly go wrong went wrong. I had dedicated the day to staying home and packing. I called British Airways to confirm my flight and was told no such name was on the list for tomorrow's flight. I madly faxed through my ticket and called her back. 'Oh, P-H-E-L-A-N,' she said. 'Yes, you're here.'

In between these calls, my parents called. I answered the phone in Polish and then heard Mum asking for me in her best English. It's the first time I've answered the phone when it's been them. So of course I told them the dilemma with the ticket (which didn't really exist).

I also asked British Airways how many kilograms I'm allowed to take with me. The answer was 20. We don't get the extra 10 that we did coming. I packed one of my two bags and weighed it. 30 kilograms. Oh-oh! I realised I was going to have to leave a lot of things and get them sent. By now the time was getting on and I was starting to worry more about my speech at Rotary that night so couldn't concentrate on packing.

Once at Rotary we sat at the table we always sit at and got the coke we always drink. I, with my heavy-laden blazer full of badges, leaned over the table and knocked over onto my lap a glass full of coke. Brilliant! In just a few minutes I was due to stand up in front of the club and deliver my speech and it looked like I'd wet myself. I raced to the bathroom and washed the pants with water then dried them under the hand dryer. Not perfect but OK.

SPEECH TO WARSAW ROTARY CLUB: 13-1-99

[delivered in Polish and translated from Jennifer's script]

My year in Poland unfortunately has ended.
But what a year it was!
When I arrived in Poland in January, I had four objectives:

Firstly, to live in a country of a different culture and learn the language of that country from scratch.
Secondly, to find out more about myself. Who am I? What do I want in life? And how shall I experience various situations?
Thirdly, to travel – to see the world and learn how it works, how other people live and how it used to be in the past.
And finally, fourthly, tell people about Australia.

During the first two weeks in Poland, I spent some time in a TV studio and watched a program called 'ALL OR NOTHING'. 'All or Nothing' became a motto of my one-year visit to Poland. And thanks to that motto I have accomplished my objectives.

Firstly, I lived in Poland and can now communicate in Polish. Before leaving for Poland, I knew only a few words:

> Good morning
> My name is Jennifer
> I am from Australia
> 1, 2, 3, 4, 5
> Goodbye!

There are people who believe that before leaving for a new country you have to know the language of that country. But for me it was an interesting shock – to find myself in a place where everyone speaks a language I have never heard before. I shall continue learning Polish in Australia to be able to work at the Olympics in Sydney in the year 2000.

I got to know the Polish culture through all my senses: taste, hearing, sight, touch and smell. I love Polish food; I shall miss *krupnik* [barley soup], *pierogi* [dumplings], *bigos* [stew], *kiełbasa* [sausage], *paczki* [doughnuts]... etc. I ate a lot and worry a bit, as I shall get back to Australia when it is summer, and I am now a bit fatter and have a white skin!

I also like Polish music – both contemporary and old. I went to a few concerts in Warsaw and saw such performers as Kult, Grosik and Katarzyna Goniec. I love Polish folk music. For the whole year I was a member of a folk band called Promni attending rehearsals each Thursday and even performed for Polish television. We did a special show for Whitsunday.

In Australia we have a lot of cultures, as people arrived from all over the world. Now it was very interesting for me to live in a country of only one culture. Changing seasons were also a novelty for me. In my town, near Sydney, we also have four seasons but not the same as in Europe. We do not have snow, and in summer 35 degrees is normal. I spent the whole twelve months in Poland, and that means that I saw the Polish landscape in all the seasons. I watched how people's moods change in different seasons. A depression in winter and a joy in summer!

Secondly, I learned a lot about myself. Also, a lot of things changed in my life: my childhood ended, and adulthood started. In Poland too, many things changed: NATO, EU, privatisation, etc. During that turbulent period for me I looked for and found answers to questions such as: Who am I? What do I want in life? And how shall I experience various situations? Now I know that I am an Australian who likes independence, variety and travel. I know that I want to be an architect. This year I saw many buildings and I am very happy that I studied one semester at the Polytechnic. I now know that I can manage without my parents and make contacts in a new language. I worked as a counsellor at a children's camp and a children's teacher. It was something new for me and gave me a lot of satisfaction.

Thirdly, I was lucky to have a chance to travel a lot. It was great to see other places and experience new things. I organised itineraries, tickets, money, etc. myself. Cooperation with friends was also important, and once I had to get back on my own because a friend did not have a visa!

In Poland I visited:

> Krakow with my family
> Sopot, Gdansk and Gdynia with my school
> Torun at a Rotary meeting
> Lublin and Zamosc with the Rotary youth
> the Masurian Lakes with my school
> the Beskidy Mountains on a camp for children where I was a children's
>   counsellor
> the Baltic Sea with my friend's family
> Zelazowa Wola.

As for abroad, I visited:

> England, Ireland, France and Spain with exchange students
> Prague with a school excursion
> Italy with my friend from Australia in summer
> Budapest with my English friends
> Stockholm with my exchange colleague
> Austria twice, with Mr Novak. This is where I spent a wonderful Christmas.

And finally, fourthly, I had lots of opportunities to tell people about Australia. Most Poles know that there are kangaroos in Australia and, if anything else, that koalas eat eucalyptus leaves and fall down the trees! There is however, more to Australia than just kangaroos and drunken koalas! I shared my culture, especially at school, with families who hosted me and with children at the camp. At school, in my class I gave a few speeches on Australia. I also wrote a few articles in the school magazine. I spoke with host parents about my country, showed them photos, we listened to Australian music, and I prepared Australian meals. At the summer camp I taught the children how to paint in the Aboriginal way, how to throw a boomerang and sing Australian songs.

Truly, it was the best year in my life. I hope that I gave as much as I got. It is a pity that I have to leave, but I am happy of course that I am going back home. There is an Australian song that reflects my feeling perfectly:

'I've been around the world a couple of times or maybe more
I've seen the sights I've had delights of every foreign shore
But when my friends all ask me the place that I adore
I tell them right away:

Give me a home among the gum trees
With lots of plum trees
A sheep or two and a kangaroo
A clothesline out the back
Veranda out the front
And an old rocking chair!'

I am sure that I shall visit Poland once again. Thank you so much for an interesting year '98 which was facilitated by the Warsaw Rotary Club and the families with whom I lived. I hope that many more exchange students will fall in love with Poland the way I did.

My speech was very well received. They applauded at the part where I said I would continue studying Polish in Australia in the hope that I will be able to work as a translator for the Olympics in Sydney 2000. They also asked me to leave them the speech, which I did. They said that my speech was the best ever. In addition to the exchange students, also present were Tym, Alina, Pieter and Oskar. After the meeting Maksym brought over some champagne then most of us went to the pub (the Wednesday ritual).

I finished my packing when I got home and thankfully, even though both together still weighed 37 kilograms, they let it through.

There was quite a group to bid me farewell at the airport, including a delegation of four people from my Lelewel class. I didn't cry then, but when I got on the plane to London and sat in my place, I just bawled.

Flying Home

15-1-99

'Some day we'll all be together once more
When all the ships will come back to the shore
I realised something I'd known from before
I still call Australia home.'
[Peter Allen, 'I Still Call Australia Home']

I'm really excited about going home now. Most of us exchange students are sitting together on the plane and we've hardly stopped talking about our experiences. I'm really glad I kept this diary all year because I believe that if I am to share my story it will be most successful through the written medium.

AFTERWORD

On her return to Australia in January 1999 Jennifer commenced her university studies at the University of Newcastle, NSW. She achieved the Bachelor of Architecture with First Class Honours and continued studying, achieving her Master of Environment and Business Management in 2015. She had a successful career as a Project Manager for the NSW Government.

Daniel's proposal of marriage was indeed sincere, and Jennifer's promise to give him an answer in two years' time was also honoured. On her visit to Brazil in the summer of 2000/2001, Jennifer and Daniel became engaged. However, after a further two years of living apart while studying, they both accepted that their respective homelands of Australia and Brazil were too important to forgo, and their relationship ended. In the box of Jennifer's Poland memorabilia, I found the shell she described on 7 October, the one that she and Daniel pulled apart on the beach in Sopot. The shell, with Baltic sand still sticking to it, was in a small box together with her engagement ring. It was this shell that was used by Dayna Perez for the illustration in this publication.

Agnieszka remained one of Jennifer's closest friends. In 2009 Jennifer was an attendant at her wedding in Warsaw, and together we grieved when I visited Warsaw in 2019. Among my luggage for that visit was the treasured number 18 tram sign, signed by Jennifer's friends for her eighteenth birthday, that I returned to its home town.

Jennifer eventually found the man of her dreams when working in Sydney and together they established their careers in Newcastle, NSW. The desire for travel and opportunities for new experiences, inspired by her year in Poland, continued throughout Jennifer's life. In 2008 in the Philippines, and again in 2014 in Bhutan, Jennifer lived for a year away from home, each time as a volunteer for development for the Australian government. With her husband, also a keen traveller and hiker, she often spent time in the Bhutanese Himalayas while living in Thimphu. And so the prediction she made on 19 April 1998, having watched the film *Seven Years in Tibet,* was happily fulfilled:

> ...*after the beautiful scenery of the Himalayas I want to go climbing there. One day I will.*

During each of these subsequent years overseas Jennifer recorded her experiences. In keeping with technological advancement, these diaries took the form of a blog, and are published on-line:

http://jeninthephilippines.blogspot.com

https://jeninbhutan.wordpress.com

Perhaps the most unsettling statements made by Jennifer in this diary are her references to Wednesdays:

> *I told you things always go wrong on Wednesday.*

Jennifer's tragic death occurred on a Wednesday as she rode her Vespa to work. She was 36 years old.

Jennifer was a champion of the environment, working and advocating for sustainability both in her work and as a volunteer. Profits from the sale of this book will be donated to Beyond Zero Emissions (https://bze.org.au) in her honour.

Eighteen was indeed a pivotal year for Jennifer. It not only marked the commencement of adulthood, independence and the love of travel, but also the half-way point of her life. I am forever grateful that she fulfilled her ultimate achievement.

Kathryn R Bennett

" If I can live my whole life
thinking each day,

*If I die tomorrow I'll still be satisfied
in what I achieved during my life,*

then I think I will have reached
the ultimate achievement.

Jennifer C Phelan
30 October 1998 "

Lightning Source UK Ltd.
Milton Keynes UK
UKHW041314281022
411260UK00008B/330